Endorsemen

Cheryl tells a compelling story of love, loss, and finding freedom during one of the most difficult times in her life. By weaving together events related to her role as a caregiver with events from her past, she gives the reader a path for finding peace during riveting change and personal transition.

—**Henna Inam**,
CEO, Transformational Leadership Inc.

I found *Hang on Tight. Pray* to be a wonderful work of love, as Cheryl took me on her journey to peace. In it she highlights the challenge presented by end-of-life decisions. Additionally, she examines the issues and the obstacles of our modern-day health care system – concerns that one never seems able to prepare for. Cheryl also explores the complexity of the mother-daughter relationship, the process of saying goodbye, and coming to terms with loss. I would recommend this book to anyone facing the end-of-life care of a loved one, as it may help in finding peace.

—**Jennifer Barnett**,
Registered Nurse, retired

Cheryl Jordan weaves a thread through an amazing recollection of childhood, experiences, exhausting caretaking responsibilities for her dying Mother and a thriving professional career. Along the way she realizes that she's an empath/sensitive soul and this answers why she suffered the pattern of being misunderstood, bullied and traumatized. Cheryl details the maladies of the medical community and her fight to have respect given that her mother deserved. The reader can be inspired by her mother's battle to endure unbelievable physical pain which demonstrates the resiliency of the human spirit. The depth of love between Cheryl and her Mother became an unbreakable bond that can be felt. Her willingness to share her vulnerabilities that accounted for hurtful thoughts, actions and behaviors sensitizes the reader and awakens the humanity in us all.

—**Nikki D. Shearer-Tilford**,
Contributing Writer, *Chicken Soup For The African-American Soul* and *Chicken Soup For The African American Woman's Soul*

In *Hang on Tight*, my dear friend Dr. Cheryl Jordan, shares the deeply personal journey of her role as the primary caregiver to her mother. Over the course of the years following her mother's stroke and eventual death, Cheryl gives us a vivid picture of a healthcare system ill-equipped to handle the growing needs for holistic geriatric care, and in a way that is not surprising, Cheryl advocates for system change. Beyond a sobering look at our current healthcare system, Cheryl's memoir speaks to all of us. We get to know her mother as a face and figure reflective of all aging people making their final trek "home." And we are captivated with empathy of how this journey of caregiving leaves us knowing ourselves better and turning toward a new reality of strength, giving, compassion, peace, and hope.

—**Tonya Harris Cornileus**, Ph.D.,
SVP, Human Resources,
The Walt Disney Company

Funny, poignant, and full of grace, Dr. Cheryl Jordan's book, based on her caregiving during the final years of her mother's life, describes what it means to be an advocate navigating a public system for someone you love. Countless caregivers share similar experiences as they navigate public systems ranging from health care to the prison industrial complex where the caregivers of children of the incarcerated I have served for thirty-five years are immersed. Her compelling book shares all the living that occurs even in the starkest situations and how caregivers can navigate uncharted waters when they get in touch with their needs and those they care for.

—**Sandra Barnhill**, J.D.,
Founder & CEO, Foreverfamily, Inc.

Cheryl Jordan's *Hang on Tight. Pray.* is a loving torchlight and a must read for anyone faced with overseeing medical care for an elderly parent or a loved one. This luminous memoir captures the emotional roller coaster she rode in not only battling the dysfunction, apathy, and patient neglect at various elder care facilities as she sought quality care for her beloved mother, but Cheryl also details the inner battle she fought with her own perfectionist expectations of herself and others and how this perfectionist behavior created a barrier to her own internal peace. In the final analysis, this book is a story of two generations of deep motherly love and courage revealed through Cheryl's unwavering efforts to find and provide the best care possible for her mother and through vivid stories of Jean Jordan that amplify and honor her bravery and life-long commitment to her family and many others.

—**Timothy W. Goodly**, Ph.D.,
SVP & Chief Human Resources Officer,
The Blank Family of Businesses

Striking! Compelling! Honest! Gut-wrenching!

Cheryl Jordan plays the soundtracks of her emotions in such an indisputably intentional, yet delicate manner, that the reader dares not look away or stray away from what was, is, or will be expressed. Moreover, she displays a luscious array of intermingling yet contradictory feelings that so many caregivers may be hesitant or ashamed to embrace within themselves. Although kindness and caring emerge as centerpieces in the book, Cheryl does a wonderful job in directing the reader to insightfully examine the inevitable weakness, the ever-present uncertainty, and even the undeniable defeat punctuating the caregiver's journey.

In subtle ways, Cheryl unmasks herself as a masterful and natural storyteller directing each memory into the psyche of the reader; seamlessly and synergistically, the scents, sounds, sights, and sensations all become one with the reader. There's no getting around it. There's no way out of it.

Cheryl's depictions of her caregiving journey will potentially give caregivers permission to discard many of society's notions regarding how one *should* and *should not* feel as their challenging journey with caregiving progresses. I see this book as one of those documents that will inspire and motivate caregivers everywhere to continue on the "labor of love" highway, in spite of questionable feelings, occurrences, or circumstances!

—**Francine Jennings**, Ed.D.,
Adjunct Faculty, Lesley University, Graduate School of
Education, Division of Creative Arts and Learning

While the focus of *Hang on Tight. Pray: A Journey from Perfection to Peace* is the care of an elderly parent, this is an exceedingly useful resource for anyone at any age in the planning for the unexpected. The pearls of wisdom author Cheryl Jordan shares throughout the book allow you to quickly locate aspects that are relevant to your situation.

—**Judy O'Beirn**,
International Bestselling Author

Time is of the essence when caring for a loved one and *Hang on Tight. Pray: A Journey from Perfection to Peace*, covers a wide range of topics from emotions to end of life planning. Author Cheryl Jordan comes from a place of genuine compassion and desire to help others who are or will be embarking on their journey with their loved ones. I highly recommend this book!

—**George Jerjian**,
Mindset Mentor, Writer and Speaker

HANG ON TIGHT. PRAY.

A JOURNEY FROM PERFECTION TO PEACE

CHERYL JORDAN, PhD

Hasmark
PUBLISHING
INTERNATIONAL

Published by
Hasmark Publishing International
www.hasmarkpublishing.com

Disclaimer

This book is designed to provide information and motivation to our readers. It is sold with the understanding that the publisher is not engaged to render any type of psychological, legal, or any other kind of professional advice. The content of each article is the sole expression and opinion of its author, and not necessarily that of the publisher. No warranties or guarantees are expressed or implied by the publisher's choice to include any of the content in this volume. Neither the publisher nor the individual author(s) shall be liable for any physical, psychological, emotional, financial, or commercial damages, including, but not limited to, special, incidental, consequential or other damages. Our views and rights are the same: You are responsible for your own choices, actions, and results.

Permission should be addressed in writing to Cheryl Jordan at cheryljordan@umagineperformance.com

Cover Design: Anne Karklins anne@hasmarkpublishing.com
Interior Layout: Amit Dey amit@hasmarkpublishing.com

ISBN 13: 978-1-77482-182-4
ISBN 10: 1774821826

Dedication

To my son, Iman. You helped me believe in the magic of motherhood. From the first time I saw you, I knew I was embarking on a journey of a lifetime. Just as my mother's commitment was to her children, my commitment was to you. You changed my life. I am forever grateful.

To caregivers all over the world, I see you.

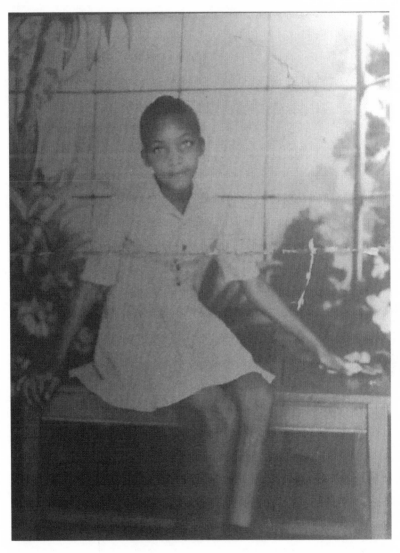

My mother as a child

Acknowledgments

Writing this memoir was painful at times, so it truly took a village for me to achieve a finished product. I would like to acknowledge my son, Iman Jordan, who encouraged me and rode the wave of change with me as I documented and journaled my experiences. His tender heart and love for me is unmatched. I would also like to thank Nikki Tilford. From the day I told her I was writing a memoir her strong desire to read the finished product motivated me to complete the book. She has been a guardian of my growth from the time I was 19 years old. I would also like to thank Justin Spizman, my editor. He helped me to create a cohesive story of love and transformation and assisted me with getting to the finish line. Finally, I would like to thank the many people who provided me with an encouraging word or agreed to provide feedback on the manuscript. To all of you, I am forever grateful.

Table of contents

Prologue

The Beast

Discomfort is always a necessary part of enlightenment.

Pearl Cleage

Every spring, we visited an amusement park in a suburb of Cincinnati, my hometown. We couldn't wait for the park to reopen to see what new rides had been added and to ride a few of our favorite roller coasters, some of which were over twenty years old. It was a remarkable experience worthy of any adult or child's wildest dreams and thrill-seeking aspirations. We would let our naturally tightly coiled hair metaphorically down and stuff ourselves with cotton candy and funnel cakes until our stomachs could take no more. We rode water rides that meandered through tunnels bright with Disney pageantry and heard music that was far removed from our reality as a Black family but that made us smile in the moment. It was an escape for us. But the highlight of the amusement park, the main attraction, was a seventy-mile-per-hour roller coaster called "The Beast." Each year, like clockwork, people from my neighborhood awaited the opening of the park to ride the storied roller coaster.

My sweetheart Jimmy and I once waited in a two-hour line just to spend two minutes with the Beast. I recall Jimmy tightly holding my sweaty hand as I shook with fear, thinking about the ride that would give me no control over the stops and starts, highs and lows, and of course, the remarkable speed that the little metal car could reach on the rickety and worn track. It was harrowing to think that we couldn't turn back; once we were strapped in and the car pushed forward, the Beast would control our fate.

While reflecting on this experience years later, I realized that the feeling I had while ascending the first hill on the Beast reminded me of the anxiety of flying I developed in the nineties. At 35,000 feet in the air, I felt trapped. I would pray fervently for a safe arrival and landing every time I boarded a plane. This unexplained and unexpected fear occurred over a three-year period of my life. Unbeknownst to me, the extreme angst I felt was related to a hostile work environment I was experiencing at the time, created by a mentally abusive manager who was never satisfied with my work. I quickly learned that I was not the only one suffering her wrath; she was an equal opportunity abuser. After every interaction with her, I was left wounded by her harsh and piercing words. Yet instead of quitting the job, which would have required me to admit that I was a failure, I stayed for two years, bleeding every day, and allowing a fear of failing to unconsciously manifest into a fear of flying to universities where I recruited for a senior management program.

As I stood in line at the airport with those same sweaty palms I long ago had experienced before boarding the Beast, I would embrace the same strategy I used when preparing to ride the impressive roller coaster that day with my boyfriend Jimmy. I tightly closed my eyes all the way to the top of the hill and braced myself for a quick and rocky descent. My eyes remained shut through each curve, hill, jolt, and rumble, my hands tightly affixed to the bar across my lap. I made no sound, no murmur, not even a whimper.

Closing my eyes helped me get through the ride that I swore I would never get on again. And I never did. Remarkably enough, this became a practice for much of the adversity I experienced in my life. Close my eyes. Hang on tight. Pray. Later, I wished I could have closed my eyes to my mom's illness. Not all the time, but during the moments when she would weep, wishing to return to the life she once had. Of course, that was impossible for me to do. So, I found myself reconnecting to memories and experiences, remembering the fear of survival, and finding solace in documenting my feelings associated with caregiving.

During this period of my mother's illness, I was immersed in a pain so insurmountable that at times it left me fatigued and breathless. The pain was intense most of the time, except when my soul harnessed enough strength to beckon a weightless existence. Closing my eyes, I imagined returning to what life was like before my mother's illness. However, it was difficult to recall what my life was once like during this journey.

Through a few stages of my life, I felt as if I was on a roller coaster journey, just going along for the ride. The Beast had given me insight into what it felt like to be out of control and simply living the destiny of its track. When I traversed a successful career, I experienced a completely different ride, one that had many ups and many downs, often leaving me unsure and conflicted. When I raised my son as a single parent, I experienced moments when I had to fight against anyone diminishing his wholeness. But each of these experiences was preparing me for a ride like no other.

You see, caring for Mom was the ride of my lifetime—a ride that dwarfed any before and left me emotionally exhausted, yet fulfilled in a way I never thought possible.

Chapter 1

Caregiver Alert

*Reflection. Looking back so that the view looking
forward is even clearer.*

Unknown

When it comes to telling my story, I struggle with knowing where to begin. So much has happened since March 1, 2016. Articulating my thoughts has been difficult, mostly because they are clouded by the emotional trauma that occurred while caring for someone whom I loved dearly but had to watch slip away right in front of my eyes.

The day-to-day moments of bottled-up happiness, which occurred few and far between, were like the elation of landing after a turbulent flight. Relief. Joy. Safety. But most of my days were filled with anxiety, fear, and pain so deep and penetrating that I could hardly breathe at times. I was not prepared for this new reality—a reality that constantly shifted and morphed into even more uncertainty and ambiguity. I had a front-row seat witnessing my mother struggle for her life and dignity while also trying to maintain her matriarchal status in the family. All this she did while using language that was permanently damaged by left-brain aphasia.

Sometimes it can be a challenge to capture an emotional journey in a linear fashion. At times, you find yourself circling back to an emotion you thought had escaped, only to have that same feeling reemerge with the seismic force of an earthquake. During the journey you realize that emotions may bounce, skip and run, while at the same time, inform your current state of being. Emotions can be a pathway to self-knowledge and be representative of the commitment we have to someone we love. So, I found myself trapped in an emotional quagmire that shook me at the core of my human existence. I would never be the same. I was faced with an aging parent who had multiple illnesses. I would encounter a journey of a lifetime together as my family and I attempted to navigate a healthcare system with many flaws.

As more and more baby boomers near the end of their lives, there is a huge gap in the ability of current geriatric practitioners and medical professionals to provide adequate resources and care. I recall a nursing home administrator with a crooked tie and wrinkled plaid shirt at a place where Mom received rehabilitation, telling me that there will be a shortage of beds in nursing homes in the coming years because of the record number of aging baby boomers and because people with incapacitating illnesses were living longer. His words added to the stress my family and I were already feeling due to the inferior level of care Mom was receiving in the facility he oversaw.

As he was speaking, I was reminded of an evening when I could not find anyone on the rehab floor to assist Mom with her toileting needs. We searched for about thirty minutes but could find no one to help. My son and I finally discovered that the aides were taking a smoke break in the parking lot. And neither of us could find the charge nurse on the floor. We couldn't find anyone from the medical team on a floor where there were fifteen patients recuperating from serious health conditions.

The long-term care administrator's comment was alarming and raised my concerns about the future care needs of the elderly. If individuals are receiving below-par care and support now, what will that mean for the millions of elderly or disabled people entering care facilities in the future? How will healthcare facilities meet patients' needs?

During Mom's illness, I heard many stories of nursing home residents being ignored, misunderstood, berated, and neglected regarding incontinence care. These were sad and unacceptable scenarios. Seniors should always be the recipients of dignified and respectful behaviors regardless of their needs. Mom encountered times of neglect as well. But fortunately, my family and I mitigated it by ensuring that someone was with her most of the time, especially because she could not always communicate her most basic needs.

Although there were many healthcare providers in these facilities that skirted their professional responsibilities, there were others who lived and breathed their jobs. They were passionate about caring for the impaired and showed acts of kindness to lonely residents who didn't have frequent visitors. They were physical therapists, speech therapists, nurses, aides, nursing home administrators, social workers, doctors, housekeepers, and food service providers. Through their actions, I recognized what I thought were desired traits for anyone working in the industry. These people gave me hope for the industry at large.

I remember a conversation with another skilled nursing facility administrator about the medical skills required to work at the facility she oversaw. She was one of the most caring and action-oriented administrators I met over the course of Mom's illness. She was adamant about hiring care providers of the highest quality, although many aides who were ill-equipped to tend to the needs of sick and physically and mentally challenged residents made it through the recruiting pipeline.

I quickly learned of the flaws in the interview process for finding talented employees, even though the administrators were trying to do the right thing. For instance, the primary recruiter was an aide with no human resource or staffing background. Further, several critical team members did not participate in the interviews. Nurse supervisors and co-workers were excluded from the interviewing process even though they were the ones responsible for either supervising or collaborating with the new employee when attending to the hygiene, medical, and emotional needs of the residents.

During my daily ventures, I found the long-term care industry extremely difficult to navigate. Medicare and Medicaid clerical workers, physicians, specialists, social workers, case workers, nurses, and more intersect to care for just one individual. If one professional does not fulfill his or her responsibilities, then the entire focus of care for a loved one often derails. Although I knew that Mom was eighty-two years old and had several health conditions, my heart and mind were not prepared for the destructive impact of a left-brain massive stroke, and neither was my family.

I have a strong desire to reveal my challenges, my tears, my happy moments, and my reflections. I am compelled to share my experiences, thought processes, and feelings as my life intermingled with the life of Jean Jordan, my mom. Having high levels of empathy, I could feel her pain, see her struggles, and read her thoughts. Her life was my life. Her tears were my tears. Her confusion was my confusion.

The testimonials, stories, and personal experiences highlighted in this memoir come from my close partnering with healthcare professionals from four skilled nursing facilities, one assisted living facility, and three hospital stays. Hopefully, through my reflections, caregivers may in some way benefit, although their experiences may differ from mine. Even though experiences may differ, the outcomes and themes of the care are the same. There is a shortage of qualified senior care aides and nurses. Only a few elderly care disability helpers will take care of your loved one the way you do—and the turnover rate in these facilities can be huge. The same year that Mom entered long-term care, the centers for Medicare and Medicaid services conducted research to gather data on staffing turnover in U.S. nursing homes and found that it was 94%. As of June 2021, the annual cost for skilled nursing care is close to $100,000 per year.

My hope is that my memories and reflections will alert the reader not to turn a blind eye to preparation and planning for transitioning parents. Hopefully, my personal experiences will give the reader a sense of what is involved in caregiving for the elderly, even though my story may vary from someone else's. In other words, my story is one data point in time highlighting my experiences, but may be very meaningful for other caregivers. My two-and-a-half years of caring for Mom also illuminates the need for more and better care and support as the senior population grows. Because of my journey through the maze of caregiving, I can provide the reader with insights to help navigate the decline of a loved one and to recognize the impact of holistic care. I will share this information by telling stories of personal opportunities, struggles, and growth.

Chapter 2

A New Reality

Dancing in the light ... but now the music is gone.

$\mathcal{M}$y journey of faith began the moment I received a phone call after teaching a business communication class at a local university in Atlanta, Georgia. I would typically talk to Mom on the phone while walking home from class. This was a special time for us to check in with one another, recap the day, and work through some of our daily challenges. But this time, before I could reach into my purse to get my phone to dial Mom's number, the phone began to ring. It was Ms. Bea, a cherished friend of Mom's for over thirty years. "Cheryl," she said calmly, "I was talking to your mom on the telephone and suddenly she was silent. Then she started speaking gibberish. I called her name several times, but she did not respond. I told her to hang up the phone. I then called the paramedics. I believe Karen and Rick are on their way to meet her at the hospital."

My heart sank. The students surrounding me on their way to class seemed to vanish into thin air. I was alone with my thoughts and in a state of shock. I dropped my purse and school supplies and tried to catch my breath. It felt like time stood still for those few seconds. After processing the call, I quickly shifted to action mode. While briskly crossing the street, I observed students rushing to catch the university shuttle. Darting in and out of the crowd, I realized that what I avoided discussing with my mom on several occasions was now a reality.

After just a few more seconds, I found the strength to take my first step in the direction of my loft. Several seconds later I called my sister-in-law, who shared a few more details of Mom's condition. It did not sound good. I was breathless again but managed to take several more steps, getting closer to home. My memory of walking through the park, where people of all ages and races convened to play chess that evening, was gone. I made it home without seeing the homeless people that typically cause my heart to silently weep and without feeling the concrete underneath my feet in the downtown public park. I did not see the cascading water fountains on Peachtree Street or the stately court of appeals building across the street from where I lived. A moment of tremendous change had already begun to alter my reality. I knew deep inside that the past was the past and the future would soon be an uphill battle of transition. As I write this memoir, my thoughts about that evening remain fleeting and blurred.

Luckily, a good friend offered to watch my dog while I traveled to tend to my mother. This friend immediately came by to try to help settle my mind and ensure that I responded logically to Mom's condition. She was a kind soul, responding to the panic in my voice. My friend was there for me during one of the most trying times in my life, and for that, I will always be in debt to her. I am grateful that she loved me enough to stand by my side that night. She was a committed friend when I was struggling to make sense of what was happening. Her actions to guide and protect me were swift and in sync with what my heart needed at the time.

As I made flight reservations and packed my clothes, I experienced countless emotions and varying degrees of panic. I was preoccupied with questions: How will Mom look? Will she die before I get there? Will she know me? I was able to successfully navigate the busiest airport in the world the next morning, but I don't even remember boarding the plane or even the flight itself. My guess is that universal consciousness was blocking any additional actions that could agitate me. God knew that landing that day was a launching pad for a spiritual awakening for me and a new beginning that would take every mental, physical, and emotional fiber of my being to survive.

I arrived in Cincinnati late in the afternoon, sleep deprived and in a state of frenzy after being up most of the night. Typically, my visits home were celebratory in nature. Sometimes I drove and sometimes I flew. When I did drive, preparing for the trip was an opportunity for me to blast my CDs, singing along to the sweet melodies of Whitney Houston and Yolanda Adams, and listening to jazz greats like John Coltrane and Johnny Hartman. Loading up on Twizzlers and iced tea, I would ascend and descend the hills of Tennessee and Kentucky, knowing that once I made it to Jellico, Tennessee, I was halfway to Mom's embrace. The mountainous views on the way were serene and scary at the same time. I was traveling alone through rural areas where I knew Black Yankees were forbidden. Having been attacked verbally and physically as a young adult because of my race and knowing the historical ravaging of Black lives, I was careful not to draw attention to myself in uncharted territory. Singing with Donny

Hathaway made me forget all my worries for a moment, but the uncomfortable feeling and thought of potentially becoming a missing person cropped up in my mind every now and then, partly because I knew someone who never made it home alive after traveling through Kentucky.

This time, the visit was different. No Twizzlers or Whitney. It was a short and emotional flight. It felt like it went by in a flash, mostly because I zoned out while staring through the oval window into the clouds. After I navigated through the airport and exited onto the street, I could feel the change in temperature. A close family friend picked me up from the airport and immediately drove me to the hospital. The day was overcast, the sky matching my sadness. Fifteen years before, I had experienced a similar feeling traveling to Cincinnati after losing a very close friend named Naomi. Her death created epic sorrow in me and it would take months for me to stop crying about her early transition at only forty-five. And now I was returning home, fifteen years later, burdened with fear and not knowing whether I would again experience moments like the day in 2001 when I lost my best friend.

On that evening of March 2, 2016, my three brothers and I stood helplessly watching Mom struggle for her life in a hospital ICU. The day before, she had been in the kitchen cooking broccoli and laughing on the telephone with one of her closest friends. At eighty-two, she drove her 1998 Nissan Altima confidently, browsed and shopped at Dillard's and Macy's a couple of times a week, served the sick and shut-in at her church, and assertively served on her co-operative condominium board. She was a thriving, energetic, strong, and vocal woman whom we found had now lost, of all things, her voice—her ability to easily communicate her most basic needs. The part of her that uniquely made her Jean.

The days of Jean Jordan as a statuesque, powerful, and outspoken woman and a nurse of thirty-five years were gone. Her new language, such as it was, now came from a damaged portion of her brain, with a likelihood that it would never get better or allow her to return to her lifelong verbal fluency. Her quick and agile "get it done" movements were no longer her reality; she was confined to a wheelchair with limited verbal ability for conversations with friends and loved ones to communicate her needs or to share her memories.

Not only was my mom's life severely altered, but so was mine. Uprooted from my existence living in a thriving and flourishing environment that motivated me to start my own business as a consultant, I was thrown into a never-ending time warp of volatility and tumult. I was immobilized and traumatized, and I was brand new at this thing called caregiving.

For the first nine months of Mom's illness, I traveled between Atlanta and Cincinnati nine times. The schedule was two weeks in Atlanta and two weeks in Cincinnati. I drove eight hours on Interstate 75 north through the hills of Tennessee and Kentucky with my comfort treats and my music blasting, anxiously wanting to see her. I was always still excited to see Mom, even in her limited capacity. I longed to be by her side. Living so far away from her for eighteen years was difficult for her and it was always difficult for me. But she knew that I was happy living in Atlanta, and even during her illness she discouraged me from moving back to be closer to her. Her desire was for me to continue to live my life on my own terms. But even when physical distance separated us, I talked to her every day. On those rare occasions when we fought, I still checked in. She confided in me. But because I lived about five hundred miles away from her, it was difficult to remain current on the daily care she received.

In this new space and reality, I returned to the community where my mom and dad raised me. It was home, but it was no longer a community where I wanted to be every day. I was in a place where I was met with resistance and where I faced a steady stream of questions that obscured a vision for my personal journey and life, often impairing my judgment. Feelings of love, commitment, responsibility, and trust converged and clashed, resulting in disagreements with family members, sometimes with friends, and sometimes with healthcare employees. My blood pressure crept upward and my mental health took a downward spiral.

Many questions emerged during this new reality. The questions were diverse, simple, and at times extremely complex. What was going to happen to me? Would I have to stay in my hometown much longer? How long was my mom going to live after suffering a massive stroke? How long was I going to live given the stress and strain of helping to care for her? Was it possible for me to live a full and rich life with a fragmented spirit? I had many more questions. Some addressed my mom's medical state and prognosis. But in the back of my grieving mind, I knew that no one held the answer to Mom's mortality or what kind of quality of life she would have moving forward.

Doctors and caregivers could only speculate and focus only on their piece of the medical diagnosis puzzle. Many of them had trained extensively to work in their areas of specialty, and for two and a half years, I observed these physicians' desire to "stay in their lane" when caring for Mom. This narrowly-focused practice led to a traditional medical approach, one that focused on a clinical diagnosis rather than treating my mom's whole body. I understood that segmenting and isolating medical issues is necessary to help identify the broken part, but in my view, the body is an interdependent mass exchanging energy between twelve physiological systems to reach optimal efficiency. Unfortunately, that was not always the way she was treated. So, the fight continued.

My belief about this interdependency is not based on any medical knowledge I have but is grounded in the symbiotic nature of life in general. For example, Mom's geriatric primary care doctor did not communicate with her heart doctor, although Mom was connected to a wireless heart device monitoring the rhythm of her heart. I found this strange because she had atrial fibrillation, which might have been the cause of her stroke. I was baffled by these medical disconnects. To add to the mix of medical conditions Mom already faced, doctors diagnosed her with mouth cancer about a year following her stroke.

For her part, mom was reluctant to do anything about it. She repeatedly said, "No!" when we brought the topic up. My brother took her to an oncologist who recommended surgery. The family's concern was the possible effects of anesthesia on her brain and her heart. Based on a conversation my brother coordinated between her cardiologist and oncologist, the oncologist confirmed that local anesthesia was appropriate. Mom was very reluctant, but with the help of many prayers and mantras, the procedure was a success. This was one instance when two doctors partnered with one another to achieve a successful outcome. From my experience, that wasn't always the norm.

This state of existence was all so new to me. I remember the doctors at the hospital speaking with our family shortly after her stroke. As Mom lay in the ICU, one of her doctors told us that there were several options available to hasten her mortality. I was struck and confused by the doctor's comment. How could any family engage in a conversation like this during a time of grieving?

We clearly were not in the best state of mind to make any tough decisions. They call it bedside manner, and it seemed distant from this doctor's training. In hindsight, I am so glad we did not opt to take another path with a quicker ending because I would not have been able to play a part in reenergizing, rekindling, and strengthening a mother's and daughter's love for each other.

Standing firm in my belief in a wholistic treatment plan led to fluctuating periods of lethargy and forgetfulness. My current state of being was overpowered and overloaded with thoughts of not knowing and by my resistance to accepting the reality that my mom's life would never be the same. All these forces united to create a seemingly endless pit of blurred absurdities and a new reality that felt like a bottomless pit. I wished she could flee this unknown place she found herself in until her body could no longer fight, and her spirit summoned her last exhale. My family and I would become accustomed to the pain and uncertainty related to a new norm for her and ourselves. We could not escape her need for around-the-clock care. We had to fight for her dignity every day. We had to protect her in her altered state of consciousness.

The new reality was that Mom was not only stricken with aphasia, but also with right-sided paralysis. Unfortunately, she could not always control her environment and personal space. Most of the time, she was unable to clearly articulate her basic needs. Gone were the words she fluently used for the first eighty-two years of her life. She was now dependent on pushing a button for someone to help her get dressed, take her to the bathroom, and put her to bed at night. This required me to embrace a vigilant approach to her care, to stay up to date on her environment in several care facilities, and to know who was going in and out of her room. Daily, Mom was attended to by a steady stream of

healthcare workers. Some of the practitioners were kind and compassionate, and others were seemingly there for monetary reasons
only, absent of empathy and support for the residents.

The new Jean understood most conversations. She sometimes
struggled with questions directed toward her, so it was necessary
to speak slowly. Of course, she was not always aware of the magnitude of her disability or always understood the message, which
created frustrating moments for her and at times provoked a slew
of heated exchanges and negative outcomes. But even though
Mom was in a new place, without failure she could still organize
her chest of drawers, create the most sentimental and charming
moments as a mother and friend, play "Sorry" with some assistance, and understand the cases she watched on *Judge Judy*.

From a business perspective, I was able to keep things afloat
during the three years I went back and forth from Atlanta to Cincinnati. However, my income dropped significantly because of
the circumstances. I had no time for business development and
planning. Working allowed me to be creative and to interact with
people outside of my immediate circle of family and friends. Dedi-
cating almost 100 percent of my time to Mom did not permit me
to generate, and during this period my earnings plummeted by 80
percent.

Romans 12:12 tells us to "Rejoice in hope, be patient in tribu-
lation, be constant in prayer." Once I realized that Mom would
never speak or walk again, hope alluded me. Disenchanted and
existing in a different life, it was difficult for me to proclaim hope,
rejoice, or be patient. My spirituality was eventually disabled by
a chain of negative events that occurred over the course of her
illness. I had no desire to seek refuge from any church, attend
Bible study, or walk into a sanctuary and not see Mom sitting

on the right-hand side of the church at the end of the pew, close to the window. My soul was anchored in a new reality—a reality called shock. This ride of a lifetime would continue as I navigated this new reality, moving from a state of shock to heightened awareness.

Chapter 3

Progress to Mediocrity

Our lives begin to end the day we become silent about things that matter.

Martin Luther King, Jr.

Mom resided at three different facilities during the first four months of her illness. Each facility had a specific purpose and focus. She entered a rehab facility once she was released from the hospital. After the rehab facility, she was accepted into a program with a focus on intense occupational and physical therapy, with the goal of transitioning her back to her home, even if additional care was needed. The third facility was for long-term care.

We were very excited when we received news Mom was accepted into the first program to which we applied. This program used intense occupational and physical therapy to assist patients in going home after suffering a stroke. We were unsure if she was going to be accepted because of the extent of her stroke, but she got in. We lived in a gray area, not knowing what was next for her, but we persevered and maintained hope.

The rehab facility that refused to continue to work with my mother was surprised when they heard that she had been accepted into the program. Of all the places Mom was a resident, this was the most challenging and potentially helpful place for her to be. The program pushed her into territory where neither she nor the rest of us thought she could go. The little hope the first facility left us with was reignited even though we knew that Mom's stay there was limited to twenty-one days.

I was still traveling back and forth between Atlanta and Cincinnati when she was accepted into the program. I moved back to Cincinnati permanently halfway through her time in the new facility, so daily for two weeks, I had the opportunity to observe her progress. No longer requiring a Hoyer to get her out of bed, which sometimes she refused, Mom had a flicker of hope in her eyes as she worked with very skilled and committed occupational and physical therapists. Their role was to prepare her for most basic needs— like squeezing toothpaste out of the tube or washing her face. They taught all of us how to use a sliding board, which was designed to help her move from her wheelchair to a bed or car with little effort.

The most exciting moment for me was when Mom had the occasion to view her surroundings while standing upright instead of from a wheelchair. Every day the physical therapists took Mom into the hallway to evaluate her mobility and strength in her legs. Wrapped in a harness around her waist for safety purposes, I witnessed Mom's motivation to participate in an activity that inspired her. It took two physical therapists to support her through the exercise. One therapist stood behind her holding tightly onto the belt securely positioned around Mom's waist for support and balance, pushing her wheelchair behind her to break her fall in case she lost her balance. Stooping very close to the floor, the second therapist guided Mom's legs forward as she held onto the rail with her left hand. This feat was a major victory for Mom, even though

I knew that her chances of walking by herself again were slim. But my thoughts did not matter at the time. All that was important was the fact that she was making progress.

The first time I watched, I quickly pulled out my cell phone to record Mom's journey down the hall. I sent the video I recorded to family members and her close friends so they could cheer her on and uplift their spirits as well. Yet my bubble of excitement burst when it became evident that she was not eligible to remain in the program. Her stroke was simply too debilitating.

The program did help her improve, but only a little. She learned to feed herself with her left hand. Her balance returned, and she gained enough strength to pull herself up to sit on the side of the bed. There were other small signs of progress as well, but it was clear that Mom would have to move to a long-term care facility at the end of the program. So, our search for another secure and safe place for her to live began again. My brother, sister-in-law, and I took turns visiting facilities, and eventually found a place that we thought could work. If only we knew at the time that the next facility would test our patience daily.

One day at the third facility, an aide arrived at Mom's room smiling and ready to assist. My understanding at the time was that Valerie was recently trained as an aide, so I welcomed her as someone who was fresh and ready to help. She walked into Mom's room with a purpose. Her goal appeared to be to make Mom comfortable and happy. I breathed a sigh of relief. I was hopeful that Valerie's care for Mom would remove some of the doubt I had about leaving her alone. Observing Valerie, I noticed that she paid extreme attention to every detail. This attention to detail even showed up in her appearance: no wrinkles in her uniform and every strand of hair beautifully coiffed to match her lovely caramel complexion. Little did I know that my last sigh of relief was right around the corner.

Before long, the relationship between Valerie and Mom declined. Mom could be difficult at times. She needed someone to care for her who was resilient and adaptable. Mom was not abusive, but Valerie was still dealing with a new life with little independence, so sometimes Mom's need for independence and for things to be the way she wanted them to be caused a raucous. I do not think Valerie was prepared to care for a resident who recently experienced a stroke. She was regimented in her approach and pushed back aggressively when Mom challenged her.

It did not take long for Valerie's smile and positive energy to vanish. Within a couple of days, Valerie sauntered into my mother's room without a smile on her face and without greeting anyone in the room. Her look was stark and cold. She was unapproachable. Valerie even became aggressive towards me. I was stunned by the change in her behavior and concerned that she was not qualified to care for Mom, so I asked the charge nurse if she could assign someone else to my mother's care.

Eventually, Valerie stopped speaking to me altogether. When I saw her in the hallway, she rolled her eyes and ignored me. I was so overwhelmed by Mom's current condition, I decided not to address Valerie's immature behavior until the afternoon I heard her discussing Mom with other aides and in front of residents. Valerie was sitting at the dining table with two employees and a couple of residents at lunchtime. I heard her say something about Mom being difficult to work with. I cleared my throat to make my presence known because Valerie did not realize that I was within earshot. Everyone at the table grew suddenly quiet, even Valerie. I walked away concerned that an employee would negatively discuss a resident not only with other aides but also in the presence of other residents. I was furious.

Personal and professional development of young women has always been in my DNA. Instead of reporting Valerie to the charge nurse, I decided to speak with her directly, which was a mistake. She was not open to anything I had to say and showed no remorse for her inappropriate behavior. Valerie became belligerent until I told her that discussing a resident's medical condition and information violates HIPPA regulations. She got very quiet and walked away. I continued to lose confidence in a system that was understaffed and undertrained. In response, I began to walk into Mom's room every day expecting to see problems with her care.

During Mom's stay at the facility where she resided the longest, we decided to devise a tracking system to capture times when her needs were not being met by the staff. When Aunt Faye, Mom's younger sister from Shreveport, was on duty, she began to take very detailed notes. She was careful to document the time Mom pushed her call button and the time when someone finally arrived. Her attention to detail was more than I expected, but it showed her dedication and commitment to taking care of her big sister.

We kept the log inside the television cabinet in Mom's room, using the log to prove our case for inadequate care. The log was helpful, especially when I met with the owner of the facility. I was already sitting down when he arrived. I remember him walking into the small and windowless conference room with an air of superiority. In an arrogant fashion, he sat down in a chair about three feet from me, leaned back, crossed his legs, and looked at me in a way I felt was meant to inform me that *he* would control the conversation, even though I was the one with the complaint.

I looked directly back at him and into his soul. I knew the "look." I had encountered the look many times in my life, especially when someone was trying to place me in a subservient role. It happened when I was much younger and not familiar with common power plays in business. During those times, I felt like I was invited into a private club for eight hours a day only to exist on the fringe because of a governmental mandate. Living on the fringe was a very insecure position, but a powerful one as well. Inhabiting this invisible but ever-present force provided me with a front-row seat to observe the behaviors of the majority and to learn to make calculated moves critical to my survival.

In this instant with the owner of the facility, I was not afraid to fight for my mother's care. I sat confidently, knowing he would not be ready to hear the infractions I would eventually share with him. Hygiene issues, the quality of food served, my mother's long waits to get to the bathroom, even the fact that after weeks, Mom still did not have a trash can in her room—I told him about every issue.

After a few minutes of listening to me, his demeanor changed from one of arrogance to attentiveness. The "look" lost its grip and was transformed into real concern. He could not dispute the facts. At the end of our conversation, he assured me that he would investigate some of the problems I brought up. He also walked back to my mother's room with me to introduce himself to her and to tell an aide to find a trash can for her room. I felt relieved. He had heard me. At least that's what I thought. Unfortunately, we continued to have to deal with many of the same issues a couple of weeks after the meeting.

Over time, Mom developed a good relationship with most of the staff, but there were many instances where her safety was a concern. For example, one December morning, I found Mom sitting on the side of the bed by herself. The aide taking care of her that day was not aware that Mom was an "at risk for falling" resident. I reported the issue, and the director of the facility told me that she was going to develop a strategy with the rest of the staff to prevent this from happening again. She informed all staff members of the need to lower Mom's bed. In addition, they would place an alarm on her bed to alert the staff if she tried to sit on the edge of the bed by herself. Yet, ten days later, only one aide was aware that her bed should be lowered and that an alarm was to be placed on her bed. I decided to speak with the charge nurse and was astonished to find that even she was not aware that Mom was at risk for falling. Several other people on the staff still did not know that my mother required two people to help her go to the bathroom and to stay with her so she would not fall off the toilet. This issue continued to happen during the entire two and a half years of Mom's illness because of a lack of communication between the staff. There was no mechanism for formally transferring critical knowledge about the residents' needs between shifts, even though as a family, we were told that there was.

It would take me a while to realize that the problems highlighted were systemic in nature and would require an overhaul of the entire facility. I knew not to hold my breath for things to change. Raising pay to find the best talent could potentially impact profit margins. I also realized that the problems we were experiencing as a family were larger than any of the facilities with similar problems where Mom had been a resident. I quickly realized the magnitude of what we all were dealing with, but, when it came to Mom's needs, acquiescing was not an option for me.

My mother, circa 1950

Chapter 4

The Nurturing Warrior

If we stand tall it is because we stand on the shoulders of many ancestors.

African Proverb

Jean Jordan stood up to just about anybody over anything, especially when it came to her kids. She was a protective parent extraordinaire—a force to be reckoned with. Jean fought for things she thought were right, fair, and true. She did not back down, ever. But even now, the image of Mom sitting in her wheelchair knocks the wind out of me. Her stroke was beyond belief. I had no language or previous narrative to explain what I felt inside for several months after it occurred. The Jean I knew was now veiled in a cloak of multi-morbidities. Over the proceeding months, especially as she moved to the end of her life, her spirit grew weak. I thought that this was not the way it was supposed to be. My heart ached. I was torn between her living a life without walking and speaking her mind, and her fighting daily pain and struggling with her limitations.

I suspended these two images of her in my mind. She would forever be the Jean with a fighting spirit, industrious, rigid, and responsible. But now she was struggling and could not care for herself. There was a split between two polarities—a walking Jean and a non-walking Jean, an extremely verbal Jean and a non-verbal Jean. I carried anguish and fear about Mom's well-being. Not only did these emotions control my mind, but I was also concerned about her inability to verbalize her needs and the impact of her communicative ability to create and sustain relationships. How could she participate in nursing home or assisted living facility activities if no one could understand her? Mom tried to communicate even several weeks after her stroke, but it was difficult to understand her. For several months she tried hard to regain her words. I remember thinking, does she know that she is babbling? Every now and then a coherent phrase emerged, giving the family hope that one day she would regain her ability to engage in everyday conversation. But that did not happen. Although she tried for a while, eventually she began to refuse speech therapy.

I believe she was embarrassed by the simplicity of the activities the therapist engaged her in. It was far too elementary for her to relearn her ABCs or pronounce the days of the week. Then after about a year of speech therapy, she started kicking the therapist out of her room and avoided eye contact when she saw the therapist in the hall. It did not take long for me to discover that Mom was very angry about her disability. There was no judgment on my part about her resistance; I constantly put myself in her place and thought about the implications for losing something so precious. We take for granted our ability to communicate. It's the bridge to all human connection and the fulfillment of our emotional, mental, spiritual, and physical needs. I did not want her to be lonely, so I stayed close by as long as my body allowed me to.

In the initial stages of shock and especially during the first year of her illness, I played out scenes in my head of Mom as the nurturing warrior with which I was familiar. The scenes were vast and would sometimes burst into kaleidoscopic imagery in my mind. As the new reality sunk in and as I transitioned to becoming her primary caregiver, I had more and more memories of Mom being both a nurturing caregiver who made Easter Sundays special for her children by dressing us up in our new outfits and giving us an array of sugary marshmallow bunnies and chocolate rabbits in our Easter baskets to a valiant fighter for what was fair and just. These memories and life experiences visited me every day.

I saw her loving heart and liberal beliefs as I peered into the kaleidoscope of her life. Although she was eighty-four years old, she had often spoken of the energy and insightfulness that young people bring to revive old customs and traditions blocking change. I had heard her say, "He is too old to continue in that role; let someone with fresh ideas step up to the plate."

Looking through the kaleidoscope, I saw Mom as a progressive thinker growing up in the post-Depression era. Mom challenged the co-op board members where she lived to change dated bylaws from the 1960s to attract diverse potential buyers. She flew solo among her peers in support of the city government's decision to build a light rail system in Cincinnati to attract tourism and promote commerce. There is no question that she believed in supporting disenfranchised communities and she never settled for the status quo, always opening her arms to differences of every kind.

Looking through this kaleidoscope, I could see her embracing her gay grandson and his partner without hesitation, although she grew up in a time when intimate relationships between same-sex couples were forbidden. Her face lit up when my son and his partner visited her at the assisted living facility. Sitting in her wheelchair wearing a peach-colored sweatshirt that highlighted her beautiful complexion and accentuated her tiny gold hooped earrings, she leaned forward to receive her highly awaited kiss on the cheek from both young men.

The kaleidoscope revealed Mom's short and natural hairstyle she wore for fifty years, even though she received negative comments about her hairstyle of choice. One time she told me a story about a social outing she attended. Fashionably dressed, as she always was, a man approached her saying, "You are so beautiful, but why do you wear your hair like a man?" Mom never told me how she responded, but I am sure she gave him a piercing stare accompanied by a snippy remark. It did not take much for me to visualize him walking away and privately whispering to himself, "I will never ask that question again." I did not think about the political and ethnic statement she was making at the time by wearing a short afro, but I would later recognize the courage it took for her to walk in her truth, even when it was frowned upon. She was a warrior.

I reflected on her as a warrior when she intervened in a health crisis my dear friend Naomi was experiencing. My precious and dear Naomi was a ray of hope and sunshine in my life. She reminded me every day how to live a life full of joy and happiness, even during moments of hardship and pain or during our chats about our love lives. I can still hear her laughter and remember with precision the times we were at odds. But I loved her dearly and there was no question that she loved me unconditionally. Naomi knew my heart and did whatever she could to protect me from hurt and pain, even if I did not always agree with her actions.

When Naomi grew seriously ill, Mom insisted that I take her to the hospital. Naomi had taken several steps to bring herself back to health, but nothing worked. She was at a loss for what she should do next, but Mom knew.

I remember driving to Naomi's to check on her after Mom had heard the discomfort in her voice over the phone. I climbed Naomi's stairs to find her on the top floor of her old Victorian house sitting on the sofa in misery with tears in her eyes. I called Mom, reporting the details to her, and without hesitation, she gave me instructions: "Cheryl, you need to take her to the emergency room, right away."

"Should I take her to Jewish Hospital?"

Mom replied, "Yes! What she has experienced over the past week and a half is dangerous."

On several occasions afterward, Naomi would say to me that Mom's directive may have saved her life. After sitting in the emergency room for about an hour, waiting for a diagnosis, a nurse suggested I go home. She said that they would have to run a series of tests and that there wasn't anything else I could do. The attending physician also told me that Naomi's current discomfort could be related to scar tissue blocking her colon from two cesarian deliveries. I left the hospital feeling comfortable knowing that she was in good hands, but not expecting the shocking news I heard the next morning.

Mom worked at Jewish Hospital at the time. I did not know if she was aware of Naomi's medical condition, so I decided to call her at work. Because Mom had been working at the hospital for twenty-seven years, she had an extended network that included other nurses, aides, housekeepers, and physicians. I slowly dialed Mom at work. The unit clerk answered, "Three South."

"Can I speak with Jean Jordan?"

"Hold, please."

"Hello?"

"Mom, have you heard anything about Naomi?" There was a slight pause before she responded, knowing she would eventually violate hospital policy and knowing I would take the news hard. She whispered, "Cheryl, it is not good."

"What?" My mind could not fathom anything too serious. At the time we were both only thirty-four years old, even though we both looked like we were still in high school.

"Cheryl, it is not good." Another two seconds passed, which felt like an eternity. "She has cancer in her colon, and it has spread to her uterus. She was in surgery last night. But she has a great surgeon. He is one of the best."

I took a deep breath and broke down in tears. All I could hear was the word "death" as Mom shared Naomi's condition. I can still feel the sting of her words even thirty-one years later.

During her illness, Naomi spoke fondly about the forceful guidance she received from Mom to get to the emergency room as soon as possible. Mom's directive led her down a path in life where I could continue to be a recipient of her unconditional love, although Naomi received a diagnosis that no one ever wants to hear.

Mom's nurturing warrior behavior continued even after she had her stroke, even though she could not do as she desired. As Mom and I settled into our new norm, Mom would become easily agitated when she was faced with her limitations. In response, the "look" became her way to wage war against any one person or situation. In my attempt to rescue her from this endless frustration, I would offer to feed her at the risk of her giving me that Black

Mama look that means, "Leave me alone. *I* oversee my life, *not* you." I had become quite familiar with this look over the years. This look commanded respect and forced me to rethink my course of action unless I wanted to come face-to-face with the wrath of Jean. I knew I needed to back away and allow her to take control.

Chapter 5

Passing the Baton

In this world, there is no force equal to the strength of a woman determined to rise.

W.E.B. Du Bois

One day while I sat in the dining room with Mom eating and chatting with other residents, Mom pushed my hand away from her plate while I was trying to help her eat and began to cry. As each tear fell, I could see her pain was revealed. Her tears impacted me as they told the story of her life as a warrior. Her tears seemed to express the pain she felt as she reflected on her life as a mother, raising her four children to reject any stereotype that was intentionally created about the unfortunate plight and diminished intellectual ability of Black children, especially young Black males. As another tear fell, I was sure she was remembering cooking dinner for us every evening after she got home from work.

My brothers and I would rush to get home by dinnertime to find all four food groups represented on our plates. We knew there would always be green vegetables, grains, meat and dairy, which typically came in the form of butter or cheese. She challenged our palates by exposing us to food that was different from the typical Southern cuisine we were accustomed to eating when we stayed with our grandparents. At some point, the beans and rice were no longer the norm. We ate out three to four times a year, usually at Frisch's Mainliner, where we would indulge in a Big Boy burger and sometimes a hot-fudge cake. Every now and then, we were treated to a Teddy Bear hamburger with its renowned sauce, which we later heard was nothing more than a mix of mustard and ketchup.

I believe her tears at the dining table were anchored to the memories she had of mowing the lawn and painting the walls and ceilings of the house that my paternal grandparents purchased in the 1940s—things she could no longer do. With clarity, I remember when she and my dad eventually assumed the mortgage because the house was in foreclosure.

In the bubble of her tears, I could see the past pride she took in bringing the legacy of our new home into the light. As future residents of the two-story structure that was similar to the design of a shotgun house but with a stucco porch added, built fifty years ago by my grandfather, Mom and I dropped in to check on the place that our family would eventually call home. Grandaddy always ensured the yard was one of several yards on the street that included a beautiful garden. Tulips, daffodils, four-o'clocks, and pink and white peonies lined the back and side of the house, adding softness and rich colors and textures to the well-manicured and symmetrical lawn. Now, the lawn and flower beds of the place we would call home had been destroyed from neglect by previous renters.

I remember Mom's look of frustration the day we inspected the grounds. "Look at all the pieces of broken glass in the backyard," I said, standing amazed at the trash and bare patches covering the lawn. "Wait till you see the cellar!" she replied. Built with the house in the late 1800s, the cellar was the storehouse for a coal-burning furnace. As a young child, I remember when the coal suppliers ran a mini conveyor belt through two grates on the side of the house to deliver coal to keep us warm during Ohio winters.

Mom grabbed the handle to open the cellar door that was in much need of painting and was flush with the back porch floor to the cellar. "Look down the stairs! Can you believe there is three feet of ice down there?" I stooped down to see what was dwelling below and was spooked by the possibility that "Bloody Bones" would be lurking there.

According to the nighttime stories told by my cousins during my childhood, the cellar was Bloody Bones' home. When they sang about him ascending the concrete stairs of the cellar, I could almost hear the chains clanking against the skeleton's bloody body. In a state of total fear, I would tell myself, it is just a story. But every time they sang *Bloody Bones on the first step ... Bloody Bones on the second step ... Bloody Bones on the third step...* I could feel my stomach tightening and the certainty that I was about to shake the very foundation of 6013 Desmond Street with my scream. I would pause for a minute to escape the terror and to grasp reality that Bloody Bones was not real and if he were, I was now in the hands of a warrior. Jean would not let anything happen to me. It would be a fight to the death.

The cellar ceiling height was only about five feet and now the ice rose all the way up to the fourth stair. It would take a couple of weeks to thaw before Mom and Dad could buy a new furnace. Meanwhile, the interior of the house looked like a perfect place for squatters to assume illegal ownership. It was difficult to imagine how quickly the house had deteriorated after my grandfather died and my grandmother could no longer afford to take care of the house by herself. But with Mom's need to be in charge, she led the way in restoring the house to livable condition.

She was the captain of the ship, and my dad, my brothers, and I stood ready to receive her orders to restore a home that now was empty of its rich history of Black pride and excellence. When my grandparents lived in the house, they opened their doors to anyone in the family who needed a place to stay. My grandmother founded a church in the house, weddings were performed there, and Sunday teas and fashion shows were common. Because of Mom's desire for beauty and continuing the legacy of my grandparents, she transformed a dying home into a charming haven for her family. Mom maintained the property for twenty-eight years, even after the neighborhood around her began to deteriorate.

Following Mom's tears in the dining room that afternoon, I pushed her back to her room and continued to think about her fighting spirit and her passion to nurture. Mom loved caring for others. I thought about her taking care of a neighbor with terminal cancer and another neighbor battling breast cancer. Mom also placed herself in harm's way by tending to a childhood friend of my brother's after he was shot five times in front of her house. She held him in her arms without even thinking that the shooter might return to make sure he was dead and she stayed with him until the paramedics arrived. There are so many stories I could share about her nurturing spirit. She was an amazing woman on so many levels, although at times we were like oil and water.

While reflecting on Mom as a nurturing warrior, I also couldn't help but remember how I rebelled against her when I was about fifteen. As a teenager, I forgot about all the times she was there for me. She became the target of my teenage anger because of my own personal discomfort with myself. As an empath, I struggled every day to deal with the teasing and bullying that came from my peers. Mom was the catalyst for change in our family. She had to fight every day to keep the family together and to keep her marriage intact. Growing into adulthood, I realized that she may not have had the emotional stamina to be there for me in the way I needed her to be there. Her agenda focused on the most fundamental actions for survival.

Many times during those years, my brothers begged me to stop speaking my mind and raising my voice to her. Unfortunately, I was disrespectful towards Mom because I felt misunderstood as a teenager, although most family members and friends would describe me as having a "flower child" spirit. Unfortunately, at the time I did not know she was also dealing with Dad's infidelities and addictions.

Raising four children without a reliable income for several years, Mom fought for a stable life for all of us. When she decided to move us out of my grandparents' house after living there for seven years, I remember her telling me she wanted more peace and calmness in our family. She grew weary of staying in a three-bedroom house that was a revolving door for in-laws and cousins. At one point, there were as many as thirteen family members living in the house at one time.

Entering the elevator to go to the third floor at the assisted living facility after leaving the dining room, I thought about a time when Mom was absorbed in "grown folks' business," as the elders would say, and fighting to get respect. During this challenging time, I did not always see the undercurrent of tension that was fueling family dynamics. What was most important to me was having cousins close to my age to play and interact with.

My cousins took me on a new adventure every day. We traveled to the library to get books on ballet and tap dancing, and without the means to take dance lessons, we choreographed our own dance routines, singing Motown and folk songs acapella as the background music. Our hard-soled patent leather shoes left scratch marks on the concrete back porch, as we tapped to "If I Had a Hammer," and The Toys could not touch our rendition of "A Lover's Concerto." These moments brought me joy. We were a creative group of kids. We found a way to keep ourselves entertained, not knowing the tension and economic struggles our parents were experiencing.

Sometimes family members must support one another, but for Mom, the nurturing warrior, it became hell. So after living in that situation for three years, she developed a plan to escape the chaos and conflict associated with way too many people living together in a three-bedroom house. It happened so quickly, I'm not even sure if my dad knew about her plan. But almost overnight, the five of us were living in a three-bedroom, one-bath house three blocks from my grandparents' house. She was stealthy in her decisions and in the way she acted on them.

Getting off the elevator on the third floor of the nursing home, I thought about how Mom, my three brothers, and I each reacted differently to Dad's addiction. As children, we do not always know what is going on around us. Adults often keep secrets buried to protect the children, and unfortunately, secrets can generate generations of dysfunction. But despite all the negativity, my mom never wavered. She was the stake in the ground that could not be pulled loose. She made sure that basic needs and more were always met for her four children. She was a nurturing warrior, the same role I finally assumed to ensure that Mom was living her last days free of any emotional, physical, or psychological abuse.

Chapter 6

Backed into a Corner

*Yet beneath all the talk of tragedy and grace, I have
come to believe that we are destined to be opened by the
living of our days.*

Mark Nepo

Once Mom was released from the hospital, five days after her stroke, she spent time at multiple facilities to receive rehabilitation services and nursing care. Setbacks in her health typically required visits to the emergency room, often resulting in her remaining in the hospital for a couple of days for observation or staying in a rehabilitation facility that provided services to help her transition back to the place where she was residing at the time. Because she had been forced to live in a myriad of places and receive care from multiple healthcare providers since her stroke, one of my main goals during this journey was to prevent Mom's body from becoming septic, a life-threatening complication caused by an infection.

Another goal was to enrich her quality of life to every extent that I could. It was important to me that she encounter wonderful life experiences in the last few years of her life. I wanted everything for her—I wanted to create opportunities for her to feel a cool breeze against her face, so to speak. To do this, it was crucial to stave off infections that left her feeling weak, confused, and agitated, infections that are not uncommon in elderly people fighting illnesses. But the fight to create a richer life was an exhausting daily battle.

I often engaged in a struggle with nature, in denial of her condition. It proved to be a fight I could only temporarily win and only for short periods of time. In the book *Being Mortal: Medicine and What Matters in the End*, the author Atul Gawande asks a question posed by many physicians: When should we try to fix and when should we not? This question leads the person who is ill to inquire further: When do I accept my mortality and live as fully as I can in the moment without engaging in invasive and uncomfortable medical procedures that can only prolong life for a short period of time? This is a powerful inquiry. Backed into a corner by nature's powerful force, I recognized how weak and powerless I truly was. I found myself battling nature, which I could not win, and battling the nursing home and assisted living facility staff and administrators, which were just as challenging.

During this ordeal, I realized that many of these facilities operate as for-profit, long-term care businesses, focusing on increasing the number of residents and operating with a skeleton crew. Every place Mom stayed was understaffed, which led owners to rely on temporary help. Many of the temporary workers that cared for her were unfamiliar with Mom's condition. They did not know that she was what they called a "two-person assist." They did not know she had lost her ability to speak. They did not know how to put her hand brace back on after her morning bath. Some did not even know what the hand brace was for.

I did not always blame the aides. In fact, I questioned if they received appropriate training and guidance in the first place. My family and I attempted to bridge the gap by posting notes about her care. Many times, I found soiled washcloths piled up in the shower behind the shower curtain, so we taped notes to the bathroom wall about dispensing dirty towels. The housekeeper neglected to clean the toilet or the back of the sink, sparking another note. There was a note in her bedroom, reminding the aides to do Mom's laundry. That didn't always work. I began to do her laundry again because her clothes would come back full of lint or not at all. Documenting all of the infractions related to Mom's care was exhausting.

Growing up, it was not uncommon to hear friends and people in my community say, "I would never put my mother or father in a nursing home." I grew up thinking the same. How could someone put their loved one in a place where they would receive inadequate care and bed sores? I believed they were dark, dreary places where residents were mistreated by the staff. I had visions of poorhouses from the early 1900s, where rats and bedbugs infested these places. During this period, these places were meant for paupers, the infirm, and elderly people who did not have anyone to care for them. By the 1920s and 1930s, the elderly represented two-thirds of poorhouses' residents. Eventually, they were closed because of terrible sanitation and dreadful conditions.

With the discovery of penicillin and other vaccinations, society began to rely more on medications to manage illness. Eventually, we created hospitals to administer medicine and to care for the infirm. The demand for hospitals increased, but unfortunately, they could not accommodate all people with long-term illnesses because of the shortage of beds and staff. Nursing homes were established in the early 1950s to handle the overflow. Atul Gawande, author of *Being Mortal*, writes that nursing homes were created to address a problem, not to help residents who were no longer independent because of their age or medical condition. This helped me understand why I grew up believing that nursing homes were not safe. Nursing homes were created for overflow reasons; they were never intended to be a substitute for home.

Mom's multiple bouts with urinary tract infections (UTIs) heightened my anxiety and worried me. UTIs can be dangerous for elderly people, especially when they are compounded with an already compromised medical condition. A UTI can trigger aggression, mental confusion, and extreme fatigue. As the body fights the infection, not enough oxygen reaches the brain. After observing care protocols at the various facilities where Mom was a resident for a couple of years, I realized what was missing. There were only a few staff members who provided proactive care. I could see how residents eventually slipped deeper into their illness because staff members did not ask questions about the health and welfare of the people for whom they were caring.

When I was not in Cincinnati, I was not always aware of serious issues related to Mom's care. During one of my two-week stays in Atlanta away from Mom, we moved her into a new long-term care facility. I observed the clean turquoise carpet and polished handrails when I visited her the first time after the move. I immediately inhaled air void of any unpleasant smells typically associated with nursing homes. Strolling towards Mom's room, I saw several residents who would eventually become people I would look out for during her stay there. There was Mrs. Smith, who, from time to time, provided me with the latest scoop on the nursing staff. Dark-brown skinned, alert, beautiful, and with a flawless complexion, Mrs. Smith challenged the nursing staff and let me know which members of the staff were genuinely interested in the quality of care for the residents and who were not. She was my mini-informant. Another resident, Ms. Lilly, worked as a nurse at the same hospital where my mother worked. Sitting in her wheelchair with a disheveled wig and pitchy voice, she often greeted me with an extended hand and a smile. Several times, she cried about her son not visiting her or not visiting her for long enough. I can still hear her weeping as if she were a baby seeking her mother's love and attention.

As positive as this new facility seemed, I knew my mother wasn't feeling well the moment I entered her room. She greeted me quietly with a sunken, pale look and with reserved excitement. She was very weak and struggled to speak to me with her new and distinctive vocabulary. For a few minutes I thought she was dying, although I would find her in this state, later which I learned was caused by urinary tract infections, several times over the next few years. No one from the long-term care facility noted her declining behavior. No one noticed that she was not herself. Unfortunately, this scenario became the norm for the next few years. It ushered me into a constant state of stress, eventually affecting my own immune system and mental health.

At times, it appeared the staff lost track of the humanity of the residents under the guise of care. They became cogs and wheels of a very profitable long-term care money-making machine. Unfortunately, the nursing staff and aides did not observe my mother for infections. Even when Mom exhibited very aggressive behavior, no one related her actions to an infection. Most of her infections were detected because of my actions, except for one, and the only reason why my family found out that she had a UTI that particular time was because we asked the nurse what medications she was taking. The nurse replied, without knowing that we did not know, that she was taking an antibiotic. When we asked why we were told it was because she had a UTI. We were surprised and very concerned that we were not made aware of her condition.

Our everyday complaints about her care were many and constant. Some of the staff could not relate to the residents, which provoked a tug-of-war and many conflicts between the staff and the residents. Not all aides were certified caregivers. I do not know how much of their training addressed the psychological state and mental acumen of the sick and elderly but it appeared to me that they were not aware of fundamental bedside manner practices. One aide commented, in front of Mom, "Huh?! What did she say? What is she saying?" The aide's response was evidence of her low levels of emotional intelligence. She was not aware that her actions could have a detrimental impact on Mom's well-being. Mom was already sensitive about her inability to be understood.

This type of behavior from staff occurred on several occasions, eroding my patience bit by bit. I struggled to find a middle ground between patience and action. I did not want anyone to direct the anger they had for me toward Mom, which eventually caused me to stay even closer to her. Certainly, there was a better way to respond, but sadly, I never totally found the happy medium between the two. I would develop coping skills to manage but varying degrees of this personal fight would ensue until Mom died.

During our visit to Mom's last place of residence, she and I were invited to have lunch at the new facility. The dining room had open seating. Mom elected a table where a couple was already sitting. She looked very nice that day, dressed in a multicolored long-sleeved top and one of her stylish fedora hats. I wheeled her to the table where we were greeted by the couple with a shocked and unwelcoming look, especially from the wife. Mom's radar detected the "no trespassing" expression and glanced at me with a look of disgust. I knew she had a heightened sense of not being accepted because of growing up in the South where Jim Crow laws existed. We both agreed to stay, even though we knew that we were not welcome. Unfortunately, I did not realize that this was one of the first signs of the challenges my family and I would have to deal with in her final residence.

I do not believe that all long-term care facilities are bad, especially now that there is greater oversight and regulations by federal and state governments. But nonetheless, I observed major flaws in three of the five facilities where Mom was a resident. My two brothers and I constantly found ourselves in problem-solving mode because of these major flaws. Sadly, the lack of control over structural and systemic problems further enhanced the guilt I experienced about not taking her home, guilt that kept me in a paralyzed, defensive posture.

Chapter 7

The Search for Perfection

Guilt is like the footprint of a hippopotamus.

Nigerian Proverb

About a year and a half after Mom's stroke, my brothers and I decided to move her to an assisted living facility. Previously, she had stayed at long-term care nursing facilities. Mom had made some progress by the second year after the stroke. Plus, we were disappointed with the long-term care facility where she was staying. We knew she needed a change. Because she was stronger, we decided that she could adjust to a place where residents required different levels of care and assistance. Some residents were mobile, highly engaged, and still driving. Other residents, like Mom, required higher levels of assistance. Another value-add for moving her was that the facility was located closer to the condominium Mom owned and to where I was staying. I did not know at the time that this place would be Mom's homegoing launching pad.

The décor in the assisted living facility was brighter and the mood was lighter than that at her last stop. When we entered the building, the receptionist greeted us with enthusiasm and professionalism. A fresh bouquet of flowers, which I later learned had been donated by a local grocer, smelled wonderful and added to the green, mauve, and yellow color scheme of the facility. The interior was furnished with several very comfortable sofas and chairs that surrounded a beautiful black grand piano, which was located across from the dining area. Numerous residents entertained each other by playing show tunes, classics, and hymns. The dining room was also adjacent to the lobby, so as soon as you entered the building you were met with chatter and light laughter.

My family and I were excited about Mom's new space. She had two rooms now. One was large enough to turn into a small living room that we could decorate with the antique white nineteenth-century Chippendale sofa, end table, and Tiffany lamps from her home. Our goal was to create a homier environment for her.

We took Mom to the new facility so she could see it before she moved in. It was important for us to get her approval before my brother, who held her power of attorney, signed on the dotted line.

On moving day, the administrator of the facility assured my brother and me that Mom would be properly cared for. The nurse and aides on the floor told us they would check on her during the night for incontinence care. One of the more seasoned aides promised us that they would pay her close attention. I left Mom that evening feeling peaceful and energized and assured that she would have a quality experience at this new facility. I awakened the next day feeling encouraged about a new beginning for her and a reduction of stress for my family and me.

I decided to check on Mom around 10:00 in the morning and was devastated to find her in bed saturated in urine. Reminiscent of days at the previous facility, my heart began to palpitate, and my anger took over. Enraged and guilt-ridden, I quickly left Mom's room to find someone to clean up the mess and bathe her. Her first night there had been a nightmare. Self-defeating thoughts ran rampant in my head. I should have spent the night with her to see how work flowed on the floor. What made matters worse is that when I left the previous night, I noticed the aides sitting in the break room eating and watching television. They had just started their shift and they were already on break. I reminded the aide assigned to Mom that night to check on her during the night, but I should have trusted my instincts. Seeing Mom in this state triggered tremendous feelings of guilt in me.

Over the past year and a half, I had begun to rely heavily on my instincts and intuition to guide my actions. As my mother's primary caregiver, I could not falter in my duties. Remaining alert and looking for signs of neglect was very important. However, there were times when I went into instinct and intuition overload. After several false alarms, I knew I needed to learn to trust the process.

The facility administrator, the director of nursing, and one of the senior aides had committed to providing quality care for Mom. Feeling betrayed again, I was hurt that she had had to endure another night of neglect. Here we go again, I thought. My hope had been that this move would improve not only the care that Mom received but would allow me more moments of peace and grace for myself. But it would take a few more mishaps before the staff understood that the Jordan family was on the case, ready to defend our mother's honor and challenge mediocre care.

The guilt of being is a powerful reminder of the perfection we attempt to seek as human beings. I use the word 'attempt' because the narrative of perfection is created in the image of impossibility.

I sometimes wonder if the word was created to build barriers to separate people from one another. Was the word created to construct what would become an acceptable image of humanity within society that would dominate the unacceptable?

I believe societal norms dictate perfection in every aspect of our lives—how we look, how we speak, where we live, etc. The word 'perfection' is a word that I wish I could ban from human thought. Striving for perfection can contribute not only to states of personal guilt for not measuring up, but also fear, conflict, belittling, bullying, and a host of other conditions that negatively plague human behavior.

Many times, I found myself experiencing anxiety for fear of not being 100 percent up-to-speed on Mom's care. Unfortunately, this anxiety sometimes led to me berating myself. I often felt like whatever I did was not enough. Even though things got better, I continued to feel guilty about not being able to personally care for Mom. I wished I could have taken care of her at her own home, but deep down I knew that bringing her home would wipe out her savings quickly. As an empath, I would find it hard to focus on my self-care. It would be difficult for me to separate my life from Mom's life.

Even as I write, I am still working through this guilt. It is not a healthy experience. Like the Nigerian proverb, guilt can feel like a hippopotamus's foot on your back. It can make you feel like you are carrying a ton of bricks, weighing you down and virtually ensuring your defeat. Guilt feeds the darkness in our souls by destroying our light and becoming a force of torment and a feeder for self-doubt and hatred. You begin to question your actions and decisions. You also begin to look for circumstances that validate your guilt. See, it took forty minutes for them to take Mom to the bathroom. Or: If she were at home with me, she would not have had to wait this long. Look at this food on her plate, what is it?

If it wasn't enough that I felt a great deal of personal inner guilt regarding Mom, I also felt a little self-induced pressure from a close friend who spoke of his family's ability to care for his mother at home. My friend did not realize that guilt took over every time he mentioned it. I would have to remind him that our situations with our mothers were quite different. For example, my mother was a two-person assist, which meant she required *two* people to simply get her to the bathroom. Living alone at the time, how was I supposed to find or even pay for that second person? There was no way I could have taken care of Mom by myself. With arthritis in my lower back and a bad right knee, I was asking for trouble if I brought her home. Also, I would not have been able to focus on my business, which was my livelihood. Most of my clients were not in Cincinnati, which meant I had to travel back to Atlanta regularly over the course of Mom's illness.

It was difficult for me to manage my guilt. Manifesting guilt can consume your life. It can become the "go-to" when you are fearful of taking a step to reframe the story or to accept the current dilemma. I needed to learn how to say to myself: It is okay if you are not with Mom every day. It was important for me to realize that I was not the only one who was concerned about protecting her and that my way was not the only way. But I could not think clearly. I was in a trauma fog, wrapped in the fear of losing Mom. I could not see the larger context. The day-to-day care related to her mental, physical, and emotional well-being were the only things I could see.

It was 2018 and summer was coming to an end. Although the nights were cooler, the Midwestern days were still humid. I found myself sleeping longer in the mornings, eventually realizing that my body was trying to tell me something. Listen to your body, Cheryl. You have been under the spell of Mom's sickness for two years. Check your rate of speed, pay attention to stop signs, think about the toll Mom's illness is taking on you, and remove any guilt.

Eventually, with a tremendous amount of effort and focus, I learned to be okay with sleeping in late, missing an event, not returning a text message, or seeking quiet moments for myself. I agreed to delegate responsibilities regarding Mom's care to other family members. I fought for my survival, especially when I had to deal with the negative emotions and energy from others around me. Learning to be grateful for *me* became my mantra.

I am still learning to remove that guilt, something we all experience at one time or another. Guilt about not doing enough and the guilt of not being enough. Even today, I continue to murmur to myself, "No self-critique is permitted. You must take care of yourself." I know I will fight to resist this guilt for the rest of my life.

However, I learned while caregiving for Mom that simply one more day, moment, or second without allowing guilt to linger in my heart was real progress. That's what Jean Jordan would want and would expect from me. I could hear her voice during those difficult times. "Keep moving Cheryl. You cannot take care of everything." And she would remind me, "I could not ask for a better daughter." Just imagining these words from her provided me with a sense of comfort, and I am reminded that Mom continues to tenderly embrace me, maybe not with her arms but with the power and memory of her words.

Chapter 8

Fighting for Dignity and Respect

*Deal with yourself as an individual worthy of respect,
and make everyone else deal with you the same way.*

Nikki Giovanni

I often experienced a mix of emotions and thoughts during the month of August that transition from happiness to sadness, from joy to pain, and from light to darkness. I pushed my way into the world on a Wednesday, August 3 at 2:30 in the morning. In August twenty years later, my father passed away at the age of forty-five and three days later we buried him on his birthday in the oldest cemetery in Ohio designated for Black people, which was founded in 1883. I gave birth to my son on August 13, a day that would make me smile immensely, a day when seven pounds and three ounces of pure joy arrived in my life. All these events manifested happiness, sadness, and introspection. Even with so much joy and sadness coming my way in August, I was still not prepared for August 9, 2018. On that day I received a call that Mom had fallen out of her chair for the third time. Calmly, my brother shared that she had hit her head and then asked, "Can you be at the emergency room when she arrives?"

"Of course!" I told him. Surprisingly, I drove the three miles to the hospital without any fear, which of course was not the norm.

Mom had tears streaming down her cheeks and she greeted me with a look of exasperation coupled with fear as I entered her room. I immediately went to her and held her hand to assure her that everything would be okay. My brother arrived about ten minutes later, followed by Mom's hospice nurse. I was so thankful and grateful to see them both. Her nurse had been on the other side of town when she heard about the fall, and my brother's presence, as always, was soothing for Mom. We assured her that everything would be okay.

After asking a few questions about Mom's condition, the attending physician immediately ordered a CT scan, and it did not take long for the attendants to take Mom for her test. I was speaking with the hospice nurse as they came in and was not thinking about Mom's fear of the scanner. She was claustrophobic. Between the hospice nurse letting my brother and me know that Mom's admission into the hospital would no longer qualify her for hospice care and updating the nurse about the events leading to Mom's admission into the emergency room, I simply didn't think about what my mother was about to experience. To make matters worse, I did not tell her about the pending procedure, and later I felt terribly guilty. Looking back, I know that I was doing the best I could at the time. After Mom's death, I realized that I had limitations as a caregiver and had to forgive myself.

About ten minutes after Mom was taken back for the procedure, a hospital attendant informed us that she was upset. When we arrived at the testing site, she was in tears. Shaking and pale, she reached for me with a look of pure horror. Her fear consumed the room. With eyes the size of her favorite candy, York Peppermint Patties, she grabbed my arm as if she were fighting for her life. The technician said she was kicking so hard that she almost fell off the table. It is this image of Mom in this state that continues to haunt me to this day. I cannot imagine what was going on in her mind. In the past, she could always advocate for herself, but in this situation, she could not articulate to the technician how afraid she was.

Although she let the attendant know that she was not happy, I can only think of the other times when she was not able to exert her independence in the absence of her family. I think of all the times when she could not fight for her dignity and self-respect. I reflect on moments when she grappled with losing her independence. As she was prepped for the scan that day, I quickly began to massage her shoulders and assured her that she did not have to take the scan if she did not want to. She continued to speak in her own language and cried as if she did not hear my voice or as if I wasn't there. I continued to rub her arms and shoulders, hoping to calm her mind. In that moment, I realized that transition and change are unpredictable, especially if there are no guides or signs. My mom's transition from her hospital room to the imaging room was frightening for her. She had no idea where she was going, and when she entered the room, she encountered a large circular metal contraption that seemed intent on consuming her.

Many times during Mom's illness I felt I was not rising to the level of a dutiful daughter. Narratives to nurture and heal continuously played in my head. I eventually realized through reflection and afterthought that I could not control everything going on with Mom. I had to believe that I was loyal beyond measure to Jean Jordan, especially amid her current state of disability. I would have to learn not to beat myself up because dignity, respect, and independence were not possible in all instances.

I also had to accept that although Mom was at a very needy stage in her life, it was crucial for her to experience her independence. There were so many stories of Mom's courageous acts that won her respect from family, friends, co-workers, and even individuals who were envious of her desire for beauty. She always operated from a place of discipline and courageous action in extreme circumstances.

Her ordered movements for change garnered her much dignity and respect from friends and family. They also spurred a lot of jealousy from family and a few members of the community. Her desire for quality and aesthetics in life were questioned and twisted by naysayers to fit a narrative that insisted: You think you are superior. But that was not Jean Jordan. She did not think she was better than anybody; she just loved beauty and order around her and she let that be known. Her values sat courageously on both her shoulders. She knew what she stood for.

I personally believe being treated with dignity and respect is something we as Black folks should expect after experiencing the trauma of four hundred years of oppression. Growing up in the South, Mom witnessed the appalling and destructive forces of Jim Crow laws. From the time I can remember, she always fought for fairness and questioned the status quo. She stood strong, proud, and ready to fight anyone who disrespected her or her family.

I recall her challenging a store clerk who arrogantly and mistakenly accused one of us of knocking over a display simply because we were close by. Mom was no fool. She knew it was because of the stereotype linking Black kids to destructive behaviors. After saying what she had to say, she aggressively led us out of that store where employees degraded Black souls.

But Mom could also befriend anyone, regardless of race or background. Not only could she strike up a conversation with anyone, but she could also befriend an unhappy toddler on an airplane when the toddler's parents' efforts were futile. She knew how to provide firm comfort when it was needed.

Thinking about her bravery and her demand to be treated with dignity and respect, even as a stroke victim, reminded me of a story about Mom's fight to save her child's life. My family members shared this story with me again and again during my childhood. My oldest brother recalls the moments with clarity and precision. I was a witness from the womb.

It occurred on a summer day. Mom was in the backyard hanging laundry. Although I was safely nestled in her center of life, I imagine it was a beautiful sunny day, one on which a light breeze flapped the sheets and clothing clamped to the clothesline. The story goes that my brother, who was about four years old at the time, approached Mom to let her know that my brother was crying in his crib. He said, "Remember you said when the baby is crying to always check to see what is going on."

Mom ran into the house and up the stairs to the second floor where my brother's crib was to find the bedroom in flames. With his head buried in the mattress, Mom quickly swooped my brother up from his bed. I was told many years later that a fan too close to a clothes basket overheated and ignited the fire. A neighborhood newspaper documented Mom's rescue efforts, even posting a picture of her with her face smeared with smoke. She was a "she-ro" then and she was my she-ro now, even sixty years later. Mom's actions were not a surprise. This same act of daring and boldness would even continue to play out in her current state.

Her need for independence showed up in many ways. With a right-hand preference that was affected by her stroke, she had to learn to eat with her left hand. Frequently, she gave me a serious look when I tried to help her with a cup of piping hot coffee. She resisted my efforts and I was forced to sit in agony with my hands helplessly tied, unable to prevent her from getting a nasty burn. Mom's judgment was a little off, so she did not always understand that she could no longer do the things she was used to doing.

Unfortunately, sometimes I had to challenge her decisions. I decided to purchase a coffee mug with a lid. The cup reminded me of a "sippy" cup for children designed to prevent spills, but with a sleek and mature design. Of course, when it came time to drink a cup of coffee, she did not want to drink with the lid on. Unfortunately, I was unsuccessful in convincing her that she could burn herself and took extreme measures by putting the lid securely on the cup. At that, Mom began to cry. My heart sank. Her attempt to take the lid off reminded me of her need to think things were normal for her again. Perhaps she needed to imagine that she was sitting at her kitchen table in her condominium watching the news on a cold winter day, so I eventually gave in, something that happened many times. I poured some of the coffee out of the cup and sat very close to her, helping to steady her hands as finally she allowed her lips to touch the brim of the cup.

She often found the strength to control her physical space and offered us smiles that could melt Arctic polar caps. In many instances, Mom somehow found the strength to live with purpose and intention, even during times when she was battling infections or dealing with staff members who underestimated her ability to set quality expectations and outcomes for her own care. This was her grace. Her demand for dignity and respect was palpable. Pointing her finger at you and furiously saying "No" reminded you that she wanted you to respect her wishes.

A daily goal of mine was to create ways for her to be independent. It was critical for me to imbue her with hope and purpose, even if I had to devise an action that someone operating at full mental and physical capacity would take for granted. As she began to gain her strength, Mom would take it upon herself to weed out the dead leaves of her plants. I remember one visit where I found dead leaves all over the floor. Even though the aides had to take her to the bathroom, she always insisted on washing her hands even if she was not attending to her own toileting hygiene. She directed our daily outings, telling me which direction to go in her wheelchair. She told me when to stop and when she was ready to go inside. There were times I took her on car rides like my dad used to do when my brothers and I were kids. She still remained the traffic controller even in her weakened state.

Once, Mom insisted on going outside on a very hot day in July. I knew that we would not be able to bask in the sun's rays for too long, so after five minutes of enduring the excruciating heat, I was ready to go inside. I said to Mom, "Let's go back inside. It is too hot out here." She responded with a gesture pointing towards the lobby door. I thought to myself: Oh, I guess she's had enough sunlight too. But I was wrong. She was gesturing for me to go inside and to let her have some alone time. I was not surprised; I knew her need for independence was strong even after the stroke.

Sometimes, operating without full brain capacity, her ability to make sound decisions was a little off and her expectations could be strongly unrealistic. We fought almost every night about her not wearing the same outfit twice or about her eating her food, even though I could sometimes see why she didn't. The biggest culprit was ice cream. She insisted on eating ice cream, even though several hours later, she would get an upset stomach. She did not always connect the dots, understand the gaps, or have the cognition to analyze complicated issues.

On this particular afternoon, Mom was determined that she was going to remain outside by herself. I was extremely hesitant about her desire to do so because I knew the potential perils. In my heart, I wanted to create a peak experience of independence for her. Unfortunately, the cracked and uneven sidewalks outside of the assisted living facility were not wide enough to safely accommodate a wheelchair. A slight movement of a few inches could result in a serious injury or could be fatal, so I did not want her to accidentally unlock her wheelchair and slowly roll off the sidewalk. Yet Mom insisted I leave her alone. I did not know what to do. As I engaged in internal banter about the situation, an answer miraculously appeared right in front of me. The front doors to the assisted living facility automatically opened and Phyllis, another resident, steered her way outside in her motorized scooter. She saw my dilemma and offered to stay outside with Mom for a while.

I felt comfortable and at peace because Phyllis was one of very few residents to authentically acknowledge Mom's presence, her humanity, and her need for connection. She always greeted my mother with a smile and admirably reached out to touch Mom's youthful-looking hands and long, beautifully manicured fingernails. That afternoon, Phyllis played a role in restoring some of the dignity, respect, and independence Mom sought through the power of touch, human compassion, and universal love. Phyllis built a safe bridge to Mom's need for a semblance of normalcy that I, as her daughter, could not erect.

Chapter 9

Glimmers of Hope
and Courage

*Hope is being able to see that there is light despite all
of the darkness.*

Desmond Tutu

om was quite the conundrum. As limited as she was at
times, she still was utterly dedicated to being self-sufficient,
at least to the best of her ability. Sometimes her desire for dignity,
respect, and independence also stirred up controversy. With a dic-
tatorial style, she would try to tell my brother how to put her in
the passenger seat of the car when there were very specific protocols for doing so. Several battles between them ended with Mom's
refusal to get in the car. She wanted to do it her way. She wanted
to get in the back seat even though it was almost impossible to put
her there.

Yet her desire for independence always gave me a glimmer of
hope. It felt like we had made it to the top of the roller coaster
during moments like this. Her need to be treated with dignity and

respect made me smile and reminded me of the past and of the mother who planned trips to the zoo on public transportation with logistical precision. These trips included strollers and picnic baskets and catching two buses before we arrived at the destination. Mom took her responsibilities as a mother seriously. Her every move was dedicated to the care of her children.

On our way to school, we always walked out of the house immaculately dressed even in our hand-me-down clothing. Once, a longtime friend of Mom's told me that she was so concerned about us getting dirty that the friend had to tell Mom to ease up a little and let my brother crawl on the front porch. The friend told her it was *okay* if his knees got dirty. I laughed when she shared this story with me. Her story was no surprise, though. Mom's desire for extreme cleanliness and a pristine environment was driven by her need for dignity, one that catapulted her to a successful nursing career.

Dressing her for bed at night, I often thought about Mom's courage. In many regards, she was a cosmopolitan woman raised on the heels of the Great Depression, a time that limited where she could live and how big her dreams could become. Yet, she told me she was determined to leave her home in the South for a better life. And she did. Barely eighteen years old, with an infant and new husband, Mom traveled 850 miles from Shreveport, Louisiana, to start a new life and build a home in a city that would also become her final resting place.

I think about how courageous Mom was. At eighteen, I had just graduated from high school and did not know what I wanted out of life nor where to try to find it. I was twenty-five years old before I had a clue, and it would take me another ten years before I settled into a career I enjoyed and that was linked to my purpose.

You can understand how impressive it was that my mom accomplished all of that as a very young adult.

Even after her stroke, Mom was still particular about her appearance. Most evenings, it was a ritual for me or whoever was there visiting to find an outfit for her to wear the next day. She had to give her approval.

Through witnessing their life experiences, Mom and Dad passed on the gene of courage to me. I have always fought for fairness and justice. Taking care of Mom was no different. It hurts me to see injustices in our society and across the globe. My heart bleeds when I see the dehumanization of another human being. I have always been interested in hearing stories of struggle and overcoming. At my very core churns a nearly bottomless and almost idealistic yearning to help the underdog. Even in the rare cases when I provoked the conflict, I walked away sad and disappointed in myself for creating pain for another human being.

Unfortunately, my sensitivities attracted naysayers or bullies in my younger life, but my intellectual curiosity and concern with the denigration and bruising of Black bodies all over the United States inspired me to engage in the readings of Eldridge Cleaver, Stokely Carmichael, Malcolm X, Angela Davis, Richard Wright, and many more thought leaders who represented Black excellence, literary genius, and nationalism. I must admit that at times I struggled to fully comprehend what these legends wrote because of the dense authorship, but there was something about what they represented and their commitment to the cause that alerted me to what truly mattered.

Just the presence of these books in my life moved me to connect with the Black Power movement during the late 1960s and early 1970s, even though I was still young enough to be boxed in by parental rules that sent me to bed by ten o'clock and forbade venturing outside of a square-mile area within the Madisonville neighborhood. Adorned with my blow-out Afro sparkling with sheen, I instinctively desired to be a part of something vast and life-changing for African Americans during a time of revolutionary fervor.

These same sensitivities led me to courageously fight for Mom to be treated with dignity and respect and to create more glimmers of hope for myself and for her. I grew up in an era when societal norms and historical narratives about my Black existence, my mother's and father's Black existence, and the rest of my family's Black existence were constantly shaken by absolute and extreme untruths about our value, potential, and contributions. In her debilitated state, I would do whatever it took for my mother to feel and be valued.

In my youth, I focused heavily on treating Black weary bodies with care and respect and wished for equality, integrity, and safety for individuals across the human spectrum. So, the day Martin Luther King, Jr. was assassinated, the fury and seeds of injustice housed deep in my belly began to intensify.

Just as I protested on behalf of Mom's care decades later, I decided to help organize a protest in the lobby of my junior high school the day after his assassination. Even though my tendency at that age was to be a wallflower, I rose from a semi-woke existence and helped to assemble the rest of the student body to demonstrate. We decided to meet in the afternoon. I remember the daylight flooding in through a huge window that filled most of the wall facing the front entrance of the school building. At least fifty students attended the protest, although the event was short-lived. After just a few minutes of assembling, we scattered like the building was on fire when we saw police cars pulling up in front of the school through the front doors. Click-click, click-clack. You could hear the heels quickly connecting with the floor as we imagined we were running for our lives. What was supposed to be an act of bravery quickly descended into fear. Our sudden brush with the police made me think about the fear held by enslaved people running for their freedom because of the possibility of what would happen if they were captured. As one of the conspirators, I ran to my locker for fear of discovery. I felt powerless in the face of the powerful—the police. At least that was my emotion at the time.

Unfortunately, I continue to feel this way fifty years later as Black men and women are slaughtered for simply living and breathing. I grimace knowing that some institutions are strategically in place to reinforce and inflame fright among the powerless and to halt progress and change. As a teenager, I believed the police were one of those institutions. I saw images of law enforcement in the South swinging billy clubs against the heads of peaceful protesters. I heard that a neighborhood police officer ridiculed and accused my father of stealing items from a burning building when the truth was that my father entered the home to save someone he was told was trapped in the fire, although once he entered the building there was no one to be found. At fifteen, Dad had me type a letter for him about the incident. He shared it with the community Black newspaper. His story ended up on the front page. I saw myself as another potential casualty in the fight for justice. I would not win against this institution that was not designed to protect me, so I ran like hell to a safe place in a dark hallway across from the home economics classroom.

I ran then, but I did not run from the injustices of long-term care facilities. Treating Mom with dignity and respect was my calling. Now, immersed in a healthcare system with varying degrees of fairness and justice for all, Mom's care was primary for me. Standing tall with both fists ready to strike, I personally could not allow my mother to be neglected. My two brothers and I would eventually form an alliance to fight like hell for her. I stood firmly, bound by my love for my mother. I could not and would not be moved. Mom's fight for dignity and respect after her stroke became *my* fight for her dignity and respect.

There were also times when my fight was against Mom herself. She was my greatest ally and my strongest opponent and I would have to intervene to keep her from hurting herself. Sometimes she let me have my way, but most of the time I would have to find a solution to match her expected outcome. Of course, it was challenging to balance the responsibility of ensuring that she did not harm herself while still giving her a sense of freedom. In the same way that I expected the staff to treat her with dignity and respect, I also had to live up to that mantra. Jean was the queen. Through all her tears and disabilities, she fought to maintain her self-worth and poise. Even when her health was declining, she did not give up by allowing her illness to get the best of her. She fought for her value as a human being, just like she fought in 1970 to restore the house on Desmond Street. Even as she declined, she left her mark on me. I continued to be lifted by the Black pride and power she claimed. Her ancestral shine tied to her heritage of struggle did not fade into the shadows of her losing control of the most basic elements of her personal care. I was proud to be the daughter of Jean up until she took her last breath.

Chapter 10

Existing in Permanent
White Water

*Not everything that is faced can be changed, but nothing
can be changed until it is faced.*

James Baldwin

I drove home on August 21, 2018, feeling weepy and concerned about Mom's health. She was distant and puffy-eyed
on that day. She had sat in her wheelchair with her body leaning
to the right at a forty-five-degree angle. I could always tell when
she was fighting the onset of something serious like an infection.
Since March 2016, Mom had had a minimum of twelve urinary
tract infections and five bouts of a deadly bacterial infection in the
colon known as C. difficile.

The doctor informed me that the frequency of her infections
occurred because sometimes an infection continues to hide in the
body even after taking medication. I suspect that both infections
remained in her body even when she was taking an antibiotic. Taking an antibiotic to fight a urinary tract infection can deplete the

good bacteria in the colon, allowing the bad bacteria to take over, causing C. difficile. That day, observing the puffiness and darkness surrounding her eyes and her withdrawn behavior, I knew she was not feeling well and was descending into a valley of despair.

During this battle to prevent any further damage to Mom's body, I wondered if by overreacting and trying to control her circumstances, I was naïvely contributing to her decline. An internal struggle between saving and suffering erupted inside me. Was I fighting a losing battle with nature? Were my actions prolonging my mom's suffering? What would I do without Jean Jordan? She had been my savior on so many occasions. She had walked me into the hospital when I had my son and held my hand as I endured the grueling experience of labor. Mom was the anchor in my life. When everything appeared to fall apart, she assured me that all would be okay. Her love was unconditional, pure, and everlasting. My heart ached thinking of losing her. I fought that day, just like I fought when the journey began in March 2016.

One evening while driving home from the assisted living facility, I thought a lot about this complicated dilemma. Living in a society that promotes longevity, decisions regarding the medical care of a loved one can be difficult. Being caught in the hope of living forever creates huge consequences for the patient and the family. Quality of life is subordinate to living, even in situations where living equates to daily suffering. This is a dilemma many encounter when dealing with sickness or the transition of a loved one. How far would I go with my need to address every issue with Mom before realizing that her time to meet her Maker was something I could not prevent? Pulling into the driveway, I could not stop thinking about this haunting dilemma. It was a critical decision that kept me on mental lockdown.

Nothing could have prepared me for the myriad decisions I would have to make by myself or with input from my family and Mom's sister. We had to decide what medicine she should really be taking and when to push the nursing staff on her behalf. I tried to go with the flow but that did not always work. Frequently, I experienced fatigue from swimming against the current of change.

Thinking back, I was in what Peter Vaill, a well-known organizational development theorist, calls a "permanent white water of change." He wrote about the permanent states of change leaders and employees experience in their organizations. His theories explain the muscle fatigue that happens when someone is thrown into a world of continuous and unstoppable change while swimming against the current. He writes, "The longer I have reflected on what permanent white water calls for, the more I think the ability to let go and move with the energy of the system is key."

We say, "Don't push the river." I spent most of my time pushing the river, knowing subconsciously that the consequences could be serious and unproductive for me. I was surrounded by permanent level-five white-water rapids for three years. My challenge was to embrace constant decision-making as the new norm.

Small decisions became difficult ones. For example, denying my mother something as simple as ice cream would save her some suffering down the road, but would cause quite an immediate ruckus. This battle occurred daily. Mom and I engaged in battles about ice cream during bingo, birthday celebrations, and dinner. It got to the point where I had to tell the server at the assisted living facility to stop asking her if she would like a scoop. The servers honored my request most of the time, but sometimes they would forget, and before I could stop them, the question swiftly came out of their mouth: "Would you like some ice cream, Ms. Jean?"

I believe ice cream was her medicine to experience happiness and joy. With extreme focus and using her left hand, Mom parted the lump of ice cream with her spoon like God parted the Red Sea. Mom was in heaven. Eventually, I threw in the towel. The only time I challenged Mom on her ice cream escapades was when she wanted a second helping. Not on my watch, I said to myself, because I knew she would suffer the consequences a few hours later. But how could I take her heaven away from her?

There were many more decisions my family and I would have to make. Some decisions were critical, some serious, and some related to Mom's quality of life. She now lived in a constant state of second-guessing physical symptoms, battling mouth cancer, and panicking because of a sudden need to go to the bathroom.

We had to make an important decision about Mom's do not resuscitate (DNR) order. Shortly after moving her to a long-term care facility, the nurse case manager met with my two brothers and me to discuss administrative matters regarding Mom's care. On the agenda was Mom's desire not to receive cardiopulmonary resuscitation if she were to stop breathing or if her heart stopped beating. Mom was such a planner; she knew how she wanted to be buried and the songs she wanted to be sung at her funeral. She even wrote a letter describing her joy as a mother and how proud she was of her children and the psalms she wanted to be read during her service. She kept all her wishes in a brown tin box in a closet in the dining room next to the brown cardboard box of family photos that had not found a permanent home in a photo album.

Looking through the tin box, my oldest brother, who held power of attorney for my mother, and I ran across dated versions of her last will and testament, old insurance information, and her DNR, signed by her and several witnesses in 1994. She always told me that she did not want to live her life hooked up to ventilators and feeding tubes, so it was no surprise to me that she did not want physicians to try to keep her alive in the case of cardiac arrest. She did not want to end up in a debilitating state where she could not experience the beauty of life. Several times Mom's friend Ms. Bea even reminded me of Mom's wishes. As a nurse for many years, I am sure Mom had seen many patients clinging to a thread of life, sometimes simply because of the patient's family.

We shared Mom's wishes while meeting with intensive care doctors the day after she had her stroke, but because we were all stricken with grief, unsurprisingly, everything that was said was not heard by everyone. During the normal intake process at the long-term care facility, the case manager nurse asked us if Mom had a DNR. Without reservation, my brother and I replied, "Yes." The multiple conversations I had with her in the past were cataloged and etched in my mind. So, my brother and I were surprised when another family member on the phone asked: "What is a DNR?" The nurse responded, in summary, that a DNR meant no attempts will be made to resuscitate our mother in the case of cardiac arrest. My brother and I reminded him that we discussed a DNR with the physicians in intensive care the day after Mom had her stroke. He did not remember and did not agree. It was important for us to minimize family conflict, however, so my oldest brother removed the DNR from Mom's file for a couple of days. However, we eventually worked through things as a family, honored her wish, and returned the DNR form to her medical file.

I tell this story because it was a personal decision that Mom had made thirty years ago, prior to any of these unexpected challenges. Even though it was in writing, we should have sat down as a family with Mom so she could share her desire for how she wanted to be treated during a medical crisis. I talked to her every day, and I knew she did not want to end up like Ms. Mary, a ninety-year-old resident next door to her, who was unconscious ninety-nine percent of the time. When Ms. Mary did eventually open her blue eyes, her son became even more committed to keeping her alive, even though she was on a feeding tube and weighed about eighty pounds. Several times a week, her caregiver expressed her shock about the son's behavior. Even so, she came back every day to take care of Ms. Mary, nonetheless. This private-duty nurse thought it was inhumane for him to keep his mother alive and to take her back and forth to the hospital when her feeding tube was not working properly. Secretly, one of the floor nurses shared with me the fact that the added pressure of keeping Ms. Mary on a feeding tube added to the nursing staff's overall stress.

I attempted not to judge the son because of his decision to keep his mom from dying, but it was difficult to watch. When I found myself berating his decisions, I reminded myself that I did not know what kept him from letting his mother go—what kept him hanging on. Was it too painful for him to let his mother pass away? Perhaps one iota of life was better than nothing, at least as far as he was concerned. He also could have been honoring her wishes, just like we honored our mother's wishes. Was she the only family he had? All I can be sure of is the joy I saw on his face when his mother slightly responded to a ukulele player sent by the hospice who serenaded her with ballads and folk songs from the 1950s and 1960s.

I knew Mom's fear of existing like a shell without its pearl. For most of her life, she had a need to socialize and travel. She was a small-town girl with big-city ideas, so laying almost lifeless with just a heartbeat and without a song in her heart was a possibility she abhorred.

We also had to act very quickly and make a rushed decision to find her somewhere to live when the rehabilitation facility suddenly released her. We were given seventy-two hours' notice to find Mom a safe place to stay because her insurance company suddenly terminated her benefits. Allegedly, Mom was not making enough progress for the insurance company to continue to pay for her care and rehabilitation, although I witnessed her improving every day. Appalled and ready to publicly announce this unjust action on Channel 9 news with John Matarese, a local consumer investigator, I instead wrote a letter to the director of the facility expressing our concerns as a family. According to state law, we were supposed to receive a formal discharge notification, and our last conversation with the director about Mom's status at the facility occurred three weeks prior to us receiving the seventy-two-hour notice.

The insurance company told us that it was the rehabilitation facility's decision to release Mom. The rehabilitation facility implicated the insurance company. Going back and forth was like playing a game of cat and mouse. Either way, we were forced to decide where she should go, knowing that she was charged $350 a day to stay in the current facility. Because only four to five long-term care facilities accepted her insurance, two of which were on the other side of town, Mom incurred over $12,000 worth of expenses by the time we found a facility to accept her.

My brothers and I had to switch her to a Medicare plan offering more options. We had to make the impossible decision to put her in a long-term care facility that was known to provide subpar care or to have her continue to stay at the rehabilitation facility, a place where there was some familiarity until her new insurance kicked in. Given the gravity of the situation and the nursing facility's negligent behavior, we decided to file a complaint with several regulatory agencies. This was to no avail; the system did not support our concerns. We would find ourselves stuck on a track with no way to get off.

Chapter 11

A Village of Love

Ubuntu—Because of you, I am.

African Proverb

I am blessed and thankful that I could spend the last two and a half years of Jean Jordan's life by her side. I did not have to worry about being forced to leave her for weeks and weeks on end without knowing how she was doing and whether she was receiving proper care. I knew I had to be there, regardless of the disruption it might otherwise create in my personal and professional life. It wasn't as if my mother could pick up the phone and call if something was wrong. I know I would have suffered a slow death had I not been there for her when she needed me most. It was also comforting that the rest of the family could be there as well; it would have been a disastrous experience for everyone if others were distanced from Mom during this challenging time. And even more, it would have been a tragic experience for Mom to feel—and *be*—alone.

Mom could not talk, but she could feel. She could not walk, but she could visualize a stroll in her wheelchair or a Sunday ride through the neighborhood where she and Dad raised their children. She had a difficult time feeding herself, but she could taste the ice cream as we people-watched while sitting in the car at the park. She could not engage in conversation, but every day she could look across the dining room table and greet her dining buddy with a friendly nod. She couldn't actively participate in community, but she welcomed being surrounded by a community that was entertained by singers and musicians, being stimulated by visiting artisans selling their wares, and celebrating special occasions with parties and singing.

It does take a village, and I witnessed that village come to life during my journey of caregiving for Mom. There were many dedicated and genuine people who stood by her side during her trip through the unknown. They instinctively knew when and how to show up for us. They knew when I needed to care for myself and how to protect Mom when no one in her family could be there for her. I believe that angels appear in our lives when we least expect them. There is no need to tarry or shout for them. Angels are on guard and ready to charge to the scene of trauma. I do not know what I would have done without these people's wonderful presence.

There were angels of humor, like my niece, who could make Mom chuckle and smile. There were angels who flew in for only one moment, doused an event with love, and then left, never to be seen again. There were angels that gave Mom attention when she needed it from someone outside of our family. They encouraged and affirmed her need for independence. They watched over her during the lunch hour, snuggled with her when she was close to taking her last breath, and bathed her just because they cared. I am so grateful for the community of support, the energy of compassion, and the expressions of generosity. I knew this community of undesignated caregivers and providers loved Mom deeply. I learned to embrace the fact that my family and I were not the only ones who cared about Mom having the things she needed close to her so she could feel some sense of normality as she fought the demon of illness.

I had always visualized an assisted living facility as a quiet place where residents played bingo, ate, and then played bingo again. Observing the care facilities where Mom stayed blew all my judgments about the day-to-day culture in a care facility out of the water. I witnessed territorial spats. I witnessed dining room spats. I noticed resident hazing. I heard gossip and bad-mouthing about certain residents who were difficult. I remember when a lady, whom I'll call Nancy, asked if she could join a table of about five women. I could not believe my ears when I heard one lady respond, "No!"

I began to learn group dynamics and names and I discovered who was popular and who was not. Mom's community became my second home. The residents knew me well, sometimes accepting me as one of their own. At times, when I was not around, these women were kind enough to assist Mom with getting on and off the elevator and to her room. Residents' family members even extended care to Mom. As much drama as there was, there was also a special community of support if you simply looked around and appreciated it.

During Mom's first few days at the assisted living facility, I heard the staff complaining about a resident who, at times, drove her motorized scooter too fast around the facility. One time she almost ran over one of the residents, sparking a dramatic confrontation. I heard the frustration in their two voices as they discussed what had almost transpired. The director of the facility furiously shook her head while talking to another staff member. They eventually noticed I was within hearing distance and shared with me that it was a common occurrence. They were frustrated because they could not ban the dangerous motorized scooters.

The motorized scooter driver was named Phyllis. She befriended Mom, always greeting her with a warm smile and great enthusiasm. She was a fierce and nurturing warrior who would ride around in her MAGA hat with strands of hair going in every direction. I was not a fan of the MAGA ideology, but I was a fan of Phyllis. Her love cut through political ideology and even race. She made my mother feel like she was the only person in the room when the two of them interacted. Her conservative beliefs fell to the bottom of things for me to focus on. As a supporter of great change agents like Malcolm X, Angela Davis, and Martin Luther King, Jr., I did not allow her politically divisive red hat to sway my admiration for her.

Phyllis was the resident who magically appeared outside to help get Mom back inside when she was determined to leave. Phyllis always showed care for Mom, even though some moments were brief, like when they crossed paths on the way to the dining room. One warm July afternoon, they were sitting next to one another outside. In that precious moment, I saw Phyllis and my mother holding hands. It was a moment of poetic justice for me. Mom's head nodded with purpose and meaning during their exchange. It struck me that Mom was participating in something very special, something we at times take for granted. Jean was a participant in a wonderful act of pure and unadulterated compassion.

The two of them held hands for a few seconds, eventually letting go. And then they held hands again. I could see Mom's hands trembling as she reached out to meet Phyllis's hand. In the moment, Mom explored the ring that Phyllis's deceased husband had given her and examined Phyllis's bracelets with extreme focus as if she were curious about the story behind each piece of her jewelry. I wondered about what stories Phyllis could share with us. This spontaneous moment of connection opened the door for not only love and compassion but also for exploration and curiosity. I was inspired beyond measure. It was an extraordinary moment for me as they sat outside in the ninety-degree July heat.

After I joined them, I asked Phyllis about her jewelry. She shared a beautiful story about the ring her husband had given her to remind her of him as he traveled around the world for work. With a youthful glow on her eighty-four-year-old face, Phyllis told us that she had been married for forty-seven years and loved every minute of it. My question gave Phyllis an opportunity to remember that marital bliss and it offered Mom the chance to be an active listener and to relish Phyllis's memories of love.

Phyllis's attention to Mom that day reminded me that God always sends the right people at the right time. I've heard the promise of God's provisions often in my life. In Mom's case, many angels had descended from heaven to help her. A few family members remained hyper-focused on their own issues and went for months without even checking on my mother's condition. But eventually, I realized that it did not matter that they were not committed to supporting her because many angels *did* surround her. They came in the form of staff, friends, church members, and residents.

Connie, a quick-witted, short-foot soldier for justice and fair treatment made sure that Mom had what she needed during the lunch and dinner hour if no one from our family was available to sit with her. Every time we saw Connie, a retired teacher, she greeted my mother with a genuine smile and took time to make her smile by admiring her fingernails. When Connie was not there, I watched out for her mother in return. We eventually formed a caregiver partnership that was very special. Connie fought for excellent care, dignity, and respect for her mother as well, and she did her best to visit her mother every day.

I thanked God for Connie as she stood over Mom's bed to say goodbye. Although Mom's eyes were closed and she was in a semi-conscious state, my mother slowly raised her hand so that Connie could admire her pastel-colored fingernails one last time— a gesture that overwhelmed me and a gesture I will never forget.

Chapter 12

Forever Grateful

Friendship is not about whom you know the longest. It is about who came and never left.

Paulo Coelho

Jo and Tess, two of my mom's friends, always brought cheer and love when they visited her. Mom's weak eyes lit up when they arrived, knowing they would soon have her laughing from the bottom of her belly. At times, they were the bridge between Mom and me. They both could sense when Mom needed to talk about her current condition with her peers. They saw to it that she received communion and held Mom's hand when her energy was low and her spirit was down. But their laughter brought moments of levity for Mom, which provided me with relief. With them, Mom could experience a sense of play and normality.

Experiencing the joy Jo and Tess brought to my mother reminded me of a time when Jo, Tess, and Mom came to visit me in Atlanta. I was so excited about spending time with them. I knew we would have fun. And we did. One morning during their stay, I decided to take the three of them to breakfast. At the time, I had a

2001 white convertible Mustang with a black top. It was hilarious to see the four of us awkwardly getting into the low-slung sports car. We laughed and giggled as the three of us twisted and contorted our senior bodies to get in the car. Jo and Tess each pulled back the seat belt, pushed the passenger seat forward, and aimed their butts at the target, determined to quickly land in the back seat. Mission accomplished, although it took several minutes for us to settle in our seats. Mom was the last passenger to pass the test. While complaining about how low the car was to the ground, she plopped into her seat with ease. Without an instructional manual for how to get in the car, I opened the garage door and backed out to show them the city that, for fifteen years, I called home.

It was a perfect summer day to drop the top, imagining our hair blowing in the wind, even though Mom, Jo, and Tess had embraced a short, natural hairstyle for years. Each strand of their perfectly manicured hair fought the wind. Each of us wearing our shades, we rode around metropolitan Atlanta like four teenage girls, feeling liberated, free, and giddy, the three of them freaked out by the seven-lane highway where two major interstates merge. It was a memorable ride.

I did not want to take them just anywhere for breakfast, so it took quite a while to get to the pancake house I selected. I was used to driving eighteen miles to get to work and accustomed to driving on an intricate array of highways all over the Atlanta region. Metropolitan Atlanta is many scattered towns and counties spread out over approximately 8,000 square miles, and the freeways are *always* busy. I expected sudden traffic slowdowns, but Mom was not accustomed to driving in dense traffic. Every few minutes, she asked, "Are we almost there?" She could be one of the most impatient people you would ever meet.

I eventually realized in my adult life that I am just as impatient as she was, especially when it came to certain things like waiting in line or waiting on my husband or a boyfriend to pick me up. I believe this desire to "know" was connected to our mutual need to control outcomes. After several rounds of Mom's questioning about how far we were from the pancake house, we finally arrived and continued to appreciate being with each other.

To this day, I'm still not sure what happened when we arrived home. I pulled into the garage and turned off the engine. Getting out of the car was more difficult than getting in. Mom opened her door and the next thing I knew she was sitting on the garage floor. It was not a hard fall, but she pivoted and placed both feet on the ground before trying to lift herself off the seat to get out. Instead of lifting her body, I believe she lost her leverage and then slowly tumbled to the ground like a tumbleweed blowing in the desert breeze. She moved in slow motion. It was as if she calculated landing on her bottom.

We laughed to the high heavens. Mom sat for a few seconds in dismay, slightly embarrassed but mostly just recovering from a bruised ego. She eventually turned her body to the left, placing both hands on the front seat to support her getting up. And, yes, I can still see her sitting on the garage floor and the four of us bursting into laughter that could be heard miles away. Sadly, about ten years later, I experienced her falling out of the wheelchair or bed several times or ending up on the ground because I did not correctly transfer her from the car to her wheelchair.

During my mother's illness, Jo and Tess's visits to the various healthcare facilities where she lived provided Mom with relief from the appearance of always being strong. Frequently, she attempted to share her fear and sorrow with her friends. They could provide special support that a daughter, son, or daughter-in-law could not. Sometimes I left the room when they stopped by because I knew she needed her space with her friends. And she frequently reminded me that she was the mother and I was the child. I can still visualize the "stay in your lane" glance she gave me as a teenager when I crossed the line with her. Even though she was in a compromised state after the stroke, she continued to try to control her environment.

I do not know what I would have done without the attention of Jo and Tess. My goal was to protect Mom, and *their* goal was to protect me. They were my extended family. Jo and Tess always offered small, calculated, impromptu, and, at times, powerful acts of kindness. They stepped in when they knew I was almost paralyzed from emotional pain and when I had a difficult time accepting Mom's medical condition. They fed me because they knew that, for a year, I had spent seven to eight hours with Mom almost every day. Jo and Tess listened to my anger as I passed through stages of grief and loss. They filled in the gaps without asking me what I needed. Jo and Tess just knew.

Because they knew that I was falling into a deep curve of depression during the first year of Mom's illness, Tess recommended a certified aide who could sit with Mom at the long-term care and the assisted living facilities to provide us with some respite. The aide, named Pat, provided continuity of care when my brother, sister-in-law, or I were not present. Over time, Pat and I developed a bond that will last forever. She became one of the villagers.

Pat sat with Mom for a few hours three to four times a week. She became my eyes and ears when I wasn't present, looking out for Mom's safety and care. Pat reported to me actions by staff that could have been detrimental to Mom. She always kept me in the loop on Mom's mood, appetite, incontinence issues, and her own personal blunders, which were few and insignificant in the larger scheme of things. We frequently had conversations about her being too hard on herself and being paranoid about making a mistake.

She was loyal and paid attention to every detail regarding my mother. My soul could rest easy when I knew Pat was with Mom. She was an incredible source of support. I could trust her. Just like Jo and Tess, she became family to me.

When I first met Pat, I thought we had nothing in common. But I would soon find out I was wrong. Getting to know her reminded me of the mistakes we can make when prejudging a person based on limited information. She was resourceful and intelligent. We could talk about anything. She chatted about everything from jazz to the Catholic Church she attended. When her car broke down, Pat walked several blocks to the bus stop, caught two buses, and crossed a very busy road to get to the nursing home where Mom resided. Pat had her own medical problems, but she was genuinely a gift to me and my mother. Although Mom was sometimes a little rattled by Pat's presence, I knew secretly that Mom looked forward to her sitting with her. But with a point of her index finger to the clock, Mom also reminded Pat when it was time to go.

Family members played many roles for my mom during her stay in multiple healthcare facilities. One brother was the fixer. He presented solutions aimed at enhancing her care. Another brother handled her legal and financial matters, partnering with me to ensure that Mom was treated with dignity and respect. He also treated her to field trips on Sundays. My sister-in-law read to her, helped her assemble puzzles, and brought Mom homemade baked goods that made her smile. She was her social advocate at the healthcare facility.

Lots of people checked on Mom during her illness. Their presence brought me comfort and made the journey of a lifetime so much more tolerable. My aunts, Fay and Lynne, traveled from Shreveport. Then there was Tasha the nurse and Deborah the aide, who gave Mom one of her last bed baths before she died. Deborah did not work at the facility where Mom lived but came over and helped the hospice nurse bathe her from head to toe. I knew that was her gift of love to Mom.

Mom would smile when Deborah came around. She knew Deborah always treated her delicately, like a piece of fine china. Deborah took the time to understand Mom's hygiene needs. Deborah and Mom bonded very quickly, and I believe my mother knew that Deborah was not there to get a check, but rather to make a difference.

Witnessing these acts of kindness during this otherwise challenging journey confirmed to me that compassion and love are real and not something that only materializes in fairy tales. The African word *ubuntu* describes a belief that our personal humanity is related to the humanity of others. It literally translates to "I am, because you are." In other words, I cannot be, without you. The word reminds me of the interconnectivity and interdependency of human life. In the world, our spirits are refreshed and refueled by the humanity of others.

I constantly saw *ubuntu* in action, and I received several unexpected gifts from unexpected places. These impromptu gifts helped to halt the fearful descent of a ride of a lifetime They reminded me that there was still an untapped zest for life in me waiting to be revealed. They opened my heart to laughter and the generosities that we sometimes overlook because we are so consumed with our own problems.

There were only a few occasions when I engaged in social activities without the presence of my mother while caring for her following her stroke. I remember going to listen to jazz with my brother and sister-in-law a couple of times and dining with Tess and Jo. My niece and I saw a movie and went to dinner a time or two. But these occasions were few and far between. The best source of ubuntu excitement for me was going to Trader Joe's a couple of times a week after I would leave Mom in the evenings.

Trader Joe's became a staple for me. I received so many acts of kindness from store employees as '70s music played in the background and store employees danced to the 4:4 beat. I found myself retreating to a time thirty years ago when one of my dance partners could not get me off the dance floor because of my love for movement and music. I could never understand how someone could remain still while a DJ spun "Somebody Else's Guy." Sometimes after the fifth or sixth record, I found myself abandoned and alone on the dance floor waiting anxiously for the next R&B hit to play.

At least four or five times, I received a free bouquet of flowers from the Trader Joe's staff. I developed a friendly bond with one of the employees in the store. He knew me by name. Even if he was five cash registers away from where I was checking out, Brian's "Hi, Cheryl!" found its way to me.

Why did I consider my visits to the store a social outing? The answer is that I felt valued and appreciated without conditions. There were no expectations of me. The staff bestowed spontaneous kindness on me. It was just in time; several of the employees made me smile and laugh when my heart was heavy. We "conversated" as friends, as the folks from my old neighborhood would call it. Together, we exchanged stories about our families. One employee even recommended another care facility for Mom. I believe I could have left without purchasing anything and I still would have experienced the magic of kindness there. It was a reminder that the universe knows when you need to hear an uplifting word or need to experience an unexpected gesture of compassion even in your darkest moment. Just be ready to receive it.

Ubuntu reminds me of creating communities of caring where members address the needs of other community members just because they see them. There is no prompting or asking for help. Just like the employees at Trader Joe's did—you see the need, and in the process, the community becomes stronger. Mom's community became stronger, and *I* became stronger, because of the individuals who selflessly gave their time to us. Our community became stronger because of everyone's refusal to turn a blind eye to one of their own. Mom's community lived the principles of ubuntu. Their actions translated into comfort for me and Mom. I thank all of those who went the extra mile for her care and mine. There were many others I have not mentioned, but you know who you are. Your actions made a difference. And for that, I am forever grateful.

Chapter 13

Ahmani—Seeking Peace

A crown, if it hurts us, is not worth wearing.

Pearl Bailey

He was born at 7:13 in the evening in the dead of the summer in 1980. He was my freedom from pain and doubt about my ability to contribute positively to the world. He birthed in me a new life and purpose. At seven pounds, three ounces, he gave me hope. As I held him in my arms for the first time, I found peace and tranquility. With his eyes barely open, I saw the courage he would have and the faith he would need to make it in this world as a Black boy and man. Raising him as a single parent, all the odds were stacked against him. Statistics suggested that he could not achieve, and some people, immersed in stereotypical images of Blackness, would label him as intellectually inferior. But I knew that Iman was a gift. I knew he would live up to the meaning of his Arabic name, which means faith. Faith would become the guiding principle in his life. His name would inspire him to stand up and fight so his beautiful soul could emerge and blossom. I knew he would thrive as a talented musician, producer, and songwriter and with wisdom in a society that often mistakenly assumes that Black boys are curses, plagues, annoyances, and criminals.

As a caregiver, I would eventually see the link between the meaning of his name and something that I sought daily—peace of mind. I could also feel how the power of his name grounded in faith was necessary to lay the foundation for the condition of *ahmani,* which means peace in Arabic. Finding a peaceful state of mind was possible for me. But, before I could search for and encounter this state that I knew was temporal at best, I would first have to explore the negative correlation between perfection and peace. As my desire to be perfect increased, the space of peace was unattainable for me. This negative correlation reminds me of the classic supply and demand curve I learned about in economics 101 in college forty years ago. I struggled in the class, but some of its concepts remain with me today. Achieving states of perfection and peace at the same time are costly, just like the supply and demand curve. If the demand is high and the supply is low, there is an increase in the price of goods and services. Similarly, a high demand for perfection and a low supply of peace increased the harm and damage to my soul. It was costly to my well-being. I demanded perfection of myself. That doesn't mean I created a cardinal rule that I should do everything perfectly when it came to my mother's care, rather, I carried the need to give the appearance that I was in control for most of my life. I had to perfectly present myself in business meetings, in the classroom, and when engaging socially, especially with people that did not look like me. One little mistake or mishap affected my self-esteem and would cause me dread.

Twenty-five years ago, I was asked to close out an evening ceremony and dinner for a summer program that was designed to motivate Black and Brown high school students to consider technology as a career. The keynote speaker spoke for about twenty-five minutes and the sponsors of the program spoke after her. I was next on the agenda.

Inspired by the enthusiasm of the students and the recognition they received for completing a robotics project in two weeks, I walked up to the podium. I spoke of the student success and the company's commitment to the program, but I forgot to thank the keynote speaker. I was mortified when I realized I did not acknowledge the speaker. The ceremony was a Friday evening; I shamed myself the entire weekend for making such an innocent mistake. I could not find peace of mind. I was paralyzed by the incident. It took several weeks for me to forgive myself; I had wanted my presentation to be perfect.

Fortunately, my Iman saw my struggle to find peace as a caregiver and he was always there to keep me from falling. "What are you doing to take care of yourself, Mom?" "I am going to enroll you in a pottery class to distract you from everything that is going on with Memaw." "Mom, I think you should consider taking a dance class." Almost every time we spoke, he had suggestions for me to help me find the peace that, at the time, was ephemeral but possible.

I knew it was possible to achieve equilibrium, a needed balance between both states. I had learned through my Christian upbringing that God could provide me with peace that surpassed all understanding. But even with this spiritual undergirding, the practice for perfection left very few moments of serenity. I am sure my need to be a perfect caregiver hurt Iman's peace. He heard torrid stories daily. He experienced my emotional outbursts. But because of his love for me, he would stay by my side.

My struggle for perfection touched everyone that was close to me, and I did not see the impact at the time. I remember a friend contacting me daily years ago about her husband's infidelity. Every time we spoke, I was paralyzed by her anger, hurt, and her inability to take a step forward to reclaim her life. I knew it was difficult for her to let go. For whatever reason, I believed it was my duty to listen to her repeat the same story for several months, until one morning while driving to work I began to shake when I saw her name displayed on my mobile phone. That morning I decided that I could no longer listen to her. I answered the phone and quickly told her I could not be her friend anymore. It may sound selfish, but I could not allow her to cripple my mental and emotional well-being. Was I crippling Iman? Wasn't I disrupting his peace in striving for perfection? He never turned his back on me. He was always there for me.

I learned that sometimes you must seek peace even when you do not understand why things are happening the way they are. You must walk in *ahmani* and trust the meaning behind the old hymn, "It is well." It is well, it is well, with my soul. There is not always an answer. And even when there is an answer, it may be difficult to grasp. I believe that peace and joy are interlocked. Peace is a state of being that can lead us to joy and happiness. In a state of peace, we can get rid of the internal noise blocking our entrance to other ways of being.

My life prior to Mom's stroke was a testimony of my faith. Over the sixty-plus years of my life, I encountered several perilous journeys that I eventually overcame. At the age of twenty, my faith helped me survive my father's early death from alcoholism. Losing him influenced me not to adopt any harmful habits that could lead to premature death. Faith walked by my side as a single parent.

Faith drew people to me who held my hand, spoke words of love, believed in me, and lifted my heart during difficult times. Having faith helped me find a life-changing job the day after I stood in line at the welfare office to apply for assistance. I left the welfare office on a Thursday and started my new job on the following Monday—a job that opened doors for me to continue with my education, providing me with the opportunity to challenge false and negative stereotypes and myths associated with Black unwed mothers. My faith also led me to provide unconditional love and guidance to my son. Just like any mother, I focused on preparing a child to be ready for a world that would blatantly question his worth. I wanted what was best for my child.

Iman eventually rose to become a talented recording artist, producer, writer, and more importantly, a drum major for peace, someone who, to this day, continues to write songs about freedom, acceptance, and love. Not only did my son learn to live up to the meaning of his name, but I too allowed faith to carry me through to the other side. I could tell many stories showcasing my ability to overcome life's challenges because of my faith. If I was successful once, why would I not be successful this time? I could find peace as a caregiver to Jean Jordan, although it would not happen overnight. I knew by gradually surrendering the burden of perfection, I would gradually find peace. Naturally—and sometimes forcefully—integrating peace into my life, I would hear, see, taste, and feel joy in the moment. First, I would have to grant myself grace when things did not go perfectly regarding Mom's care. I would then have to banish the dark thoughts associated with perfection by taking off the crown of perfection that was hurting me and everyone around me. Instead, I would wear a crown of blessed assurance.

Chapter 14

The Power of Surrender

Seek ye the kingdom of God.

Matthew 6:33

For the first year and a half following my mother's stroke, I realized that not only was I going to live in a new reality but that Mom had a profound new reality of her own. That reality was centered on her fight for dignity and respect. I chose to carry the burden of guilt. I understood the depth and breadth of the community of support that existed for my mother and her family, but that support was not enough for my survival as well. I failed to recognize the genuine love of family members and friends and their attempts to make things easier for Mom and for me. In the first year and a half of the journey, a destructive fighting spirit had detrimentally emerged in me, and in primitive survival mode, I fought and resisted the change that not only occurred in Mom's life but in my life as well.

I began to meditate just to cope, and it quickly grew into a way of life for me. It was the first thing I did each morning. Meditating helped me to pause and witness the marvel of Mom's gift of caring and fighting for her children. Recapturing stories from the past, I could see more clearly her organized plan of care for us. I believe that every action she took and every major decision she made was in the interest of her children. We were her heartbeat. Our wants and needs were the blood flowing through her veins. With every breath, she affirmed that we were safe from harm. She deeply loved us, and although most of us knew she loved us, I'm not sure if we were aware of her devotion to her children and grandchildren.

I no longer nurtured the divinity within me or in others. Every day, I fought to see the light in living and to accept the change that was occurring in my life. I became angry and inflexible, spiraling out of control. My dysfunctional behavior led me to resent family members, fight the staff taking care of Mom, and attack myself mentally and physically in very unhealthy ways.

By focusing on everything that was wrong versus things that were right, I plagued myself with negative emotions and thoughts. From the moment I got out of bed in the morning, my brain fell into worry. Many times, I tried to anchor myself in an affirmation from the book *The Four Agreements: Be Impeccable with Your Word.* However, my words were tinged with angry intentions that led to the diminishment of others involved in my mother's care and in the destruction of my self-worth.

Then, one day, my son reminded me to surrender to what I could not control. I knew he was right. Although his words lifted me high for a few days, I continued to struggle with my anger and resentment about not wanting to move back to Cincinnati from Atlanta. My influencers and mentors, and the progressive and liberated lifestyle I led, were pulled from under my feet. There was no escaping the tremors and cracks in my soul. My identity as someone living in a progressive Black mecca with a thriving Black heartbeat was no longer my reality.

But death and endings are a natural part of life. We cannot always escape cycles of sorrow, suffering, and discontent. We cannot outsmart death. During Mom's illness, I realized that I could not control everything and I found myself searching for a road to freedom from her current struggles. Many times, I wanted to escape and run away to some foreign land to try to erase the memory of her pain. Yet daily, I was faced with Jean Jordan. And in truly seeing her for the first time, I found solace and tenderness in being close to her. My love for her deepened at a time when her grayish-green eyes were the window to a soul wrought with fear, confusion, anxiety, and lack of understanding.

A year and a half into this journey, I learned I had to pick the battles that would lead to the best quality of life for Mom. I learned that at some point, I would have to surrender—to release, let go, and embrace my inability to control every action and inaction related to Mom's care. In the act of surrender, I attempted to deflate the impact and power of the circumstances looming regarding Mom's condition. I worked hard to redirect and release the energy I had directed toward fighting change into exploring and discovering new pathways. Just like the seedling surrendering to an early morning rain shower, I experienced personal growth when I let go. But it was an uphill battle, one of the toughest fights of my life. Even two years after my mother's death, I was still learning to experience my feelings and cry until I could no longer cry, just to drain my soul. But I also knew that I could not stay stuck in my grief.

I thought about Viktor Frankl's writings on our decisions to choose and create our reality during times of suffering and tragedy.

I knew I had the power to choose how I wanted to respond and apply the lessons I learned in my life. However, I found it difficult to let go and surrender. I struggled to realize that she was no longer the fast-moving woman who guided my life as a child.

Back then, there were moments when her movements and requests were too quick for me. She was always in action mode, and I do not have many memories of her ever sitting still and relaxing except when she went to bed at night. Mom was always up at 5:00 a.m. to catch the 6:00 a.m. bus to get to work by 7:00 a.m.

She was timely, responsible, and impeccable in delivering a service to cardiac-care patients and patients on a hospital medical floor. Decked out every morning in her white uniform and surrounded by a hint of her favorite perfume, she walked the corridors of Jewish Hospital, caring for patients of every creed, religion, race, ethnicity, and gender. She was a miracle worker to me, reinforced by the number of people who would stop her at the local shopping mall to tell her how wonderful and compassionate she was with their loved one.

Professionally, I coach leaders and teams on how to move forward, innovate, and create during simple and complex organizational shifts caused by internal and external factors. I have a treasure chest of organizational tools, resources, and certifications to help leaders become positive change agents. Yet even with all my experience in change management over a thirty-year career, I was numb, bewildered, and misaligned with the flow of where my life was moving at that point. My life had to change—and it quickly did.

I did not know what to expect day after day for the next two and a half years. I found myself in a constant state of contradictions while living in the abyss of trials and tribulations, coupled with experiencing deep love, gratefulness, and appreciation for having the flexibility to provide care for my mom when she needed it most. The challenge was to accept this new reality, but also to support Mom as she faced the biggest trial of her life. I had to give in to the speed, dips, and curves of the ride and surrender.

I often had to offer myself a word of caution during this process. Yielding to life circumstances didn't mean I would stand on the sidelines, unengaged. I knew I still had the power to choose how I wanted to respond to this traumatic experience and apply the lessons I learned to my life. First, I had to learn to simply accept. Resisting nature is a fruitless endeavor. In a search for understanding the meaning of what it meant to truly surrender, I wrote a blog post entitled, "The Power of Surrender: Accept, Redirect, Learn, and Apply." Although I did not always walk in the power of my own words, I reminded myself of a few key points from my writing that were helpful for me and could be helpful for other caregivers struggling to surrender to what they cannot control. Once I agreed to accept the challenge of surrender, I could clear my head and respond in ways that were healthy for me. My thoughts were not a recipe for success, as caregiving can be the ride of a lifetime, but my new route included my commitment to a few actions that could soften the blow of change and the new reality that was not my life.

I told myself not to resist the inevitable. The more I resisted Mom's illness, the more I tried to control it. This eventually led to numerous unsuccessful results. My need to control resulted in my blood pressure rising. I also had a short fuse. When the nursing staff made the smallest mistake, I loudly complained. I expected perfection—an impossible state. Yet I learned in time that it was important to accept these experiences as simply part of the process, an inevitable aspect of being alive. Redirecting my energy to those elements I could control allowed me to reduce the amount of stress I experienced. It was key to indulging in my own self-care. I had to learn to make myself a priority, by remembering my worth and value as a human being. I was important, too.

I thought of ways to engage trusted individuals in brainstorming future pathways for my life as a caregiver. I consistently told myself that my life was not over, and not to forget that my personal goals and aspirations mattered as well. Surrendering meant taking the time to identify the positives hidden in stressful situations. During Mom's illness, I learned to reconnect with old friends, explore old and new neighborhoods, and visit cultural venues I had not seen in over twenty years. Surrendering also meant sharing and applying what I learned to live a more connected life.

While taking care of Mom, I realized that it was important for me to share my experience, hoping my actions, thoughts, words, and deeds could assist someone else experiencing the transition of a loved one. I discovered that it was possible to imbue my life with new meaning even during a crisis. I tried not to resist what is natural and searched for new personal experiences and meaning even during a time in my life when loss and grief were profound. I would have to embrace the tactic of reframing and learn to forgive, to begin the process of surrendering to what I could not control and to find a modicum of peace.

Chapter 15

Joy—an Act of Resistance

*I will not allow the light of my life to be determined by
the darkness around me.*

Sojourner Truth

There were moments during Mom's illness when I felt as if
I was having a bad dream. The dream was vivid and filled
with loss and hardship, chaos and conflict. The dream was really
an endless nightmare. I had to remind myself many times that
Mom's condition was an elemental part of life. There is inescap-
able suffering as life unfolds. And through it all, I realized that it
was up to me to access the joy within me. I had to remember to
think of how long Mom was with me on this earth and how being
with her even in this state was precious and unforgettable.

I began to create memories of joy and happiness. I would take
her on a stroll on a sunny day, exploring the surroundings of the
assisted living facility. We laughed at the chipmunks scurrying
across the patio. As a variety of birds surrounded the bird feeder,
we watched in amazement at God's beautiful creation. There were
robins, blue jays, sparrows, and cardinals. We both laughed as we

observed geese overwhelming the assisted living facility and stopping traffic to cross the street to the pond nearby. These moments with nature were healing for both of us. As we basked in the sunshine and experienced the raindrops on our tongues during rain showers, we were invigorated by the fresh air and marveled at the scenery we took for granted at one time.

The essence of our existence sitting together outside of the facility reminded me of a blog post I wrote a few years before about finding joy in the moment. I wrote about a time I was sitting on a bench alone in a small neighborhood park located close to where I lived and I observed a brick tile that was etched with the words, "lost in the woods". The brick was surrounded by other bricks with tributes to family and friends. Suspecting that someone purchased the brick to add to the circular brick-paved path bordered by crepe myrtle trees, I was puzzled by the words. Was the brick a memorial to a family member literally lost in the woods? Did the carefully engraved words reflect the state of mind of the donor at that time? Who knew, I would probably never find out. But more importantly, where was I going with all these questions? Then suddenly I was reminded by the two robins courting a few feet in front of me to stay in the moment, slowly breathe in the air, and embrace those rare instances of play. I reminded myself that we are not lost in the woods when we appreciate and immerse ourselves in the scenes that are before us. No compass is needed. I just needed to believe in the magical moments of now.

The lesson for me that day was to stop overthinking, to let now simply be, and to stop analyzing every problem or situation at hand. Now, without knowing it, I was learning how to let the moments "just be" with Mom, while quietly experiencing the shine of her love.

Creating moments of joy also included simple gestures like bringing her barbecue chicken wings, bordering her tray table with Peppermint Patties, or washing her face and hands and massaging her feet with Vaseline before leaving for the evening. I waited for her to give me the peace sign, which was her way of saying good-bye, every time I walked toward the door.

Joy is within reach. It always is. We must recognize that even in our darkest moments, simple actions can touch hearts and bring a smile to our faces. I could see the glimmer in my mother's eyes when the sunlight hit her face. Settled in what I imagined was a forever cycle of endless pain, I began to realize that the human spirit can emerge big, bold, and beautiful. And then I realized that suffering and joy are linked—they are connected and coexist. Both states are not mutually exclusive. At the nexus of joy and pain is life. And although I suffered seeing Mom in her condition, there were numerous times when I found joy in the moment.

As long as I can remember, walks in the park have always brought me joy. Nestled between Ridge Avenue and Galbraith Road, I found peace meandering the walking trail leading me up a hill, becoming a little anxious on occasion when I passed a herd of deer. I didn't want to get too close to them for fear of startling them, especially if there was a fawn close by. For forty-three years, this path was my hideaway, my getaway, and a park where my dearest friend Naomi and I walked as mature women, engaging in adult conversations instead of talking about our boyfriend adventures. No longer in high school and with years of life underneath our belts, we now talked about our lives raising children as single parents. She and I were pregnant at the same time, so of course, we had a natural bond. Our two sons also shared a bond for many years.

Most of the time, I walked this path alone, observing children playing softball in a space surrounded by the track. The park was in a neighborhood with roads anchored by mature oak, walnut, and pine trees and homes in the mid-century design. This park was a quick escape for me; it was only a couple of miles down the street from the assisted living facility, and walking this path during the time I cared for my mother brought me joy.

Several parks in my hometown gave me peace after falling out with a boyfriend or dealing with a work conflict. One of my favorite parks overlooked the Ohio River. The view was stunning, and it made me think of the look of joy that enslaved people must have had when at last they could see Ohio across the river from Kentucky, their first step into freedom. Knowing they could still be captured, these people found a hiding place at the Harriet Beecher Stowe house a few miles up the road from the Kentucky and Ohio border. Thoughts of my people drowning in the deadly currents of the river, their remains never to be discovered, also challenged me to not forget the past and to be grateful for my life. But knowing the strength of my ancestors makes me joyful and reminds me of what I can achieve when the odds are stacked against me.

I saw this same strength in Mom, even though her energy waned as her body became overridden with infections. As a strong Black woman from the South, Mom had "the fire" as described in Sonia Sanchez's poem, "Catch the Fire."

The fire of pyramids;
The fire that burned through the holes of
Slave ships and made us breathe;

The fire that made guts into chitterlings;
The fire that took rhythms and made jazz

Mom's fire helped her fight for her life. And in that fight, I know Mom found joy. I could see the flame in her eyes as the physical therapist worked with her. I could see the glow on her face when she managed to lift her right foot about an inch off the floor or when she stood upright and moved twenty feet down the hall, even though she needed the support of two therapists to do so. Just moving brought her hope, and it made me hopeful as well. Seeing her in motion was pure joy.

What I discovered is that joy comes in many packages and disguises. At times, I thought I had to search to find joy, but I discovered that joy does not have to be found. Joy simply *is* and does not have to be always linked to an event or circumstance; I could choose ever-present joy or sorrow, suffering or living. Previously, I didn't master the art of living joyfully, but I do know now that I must be committed to certain steps in order to experience joy.

Entrenched in Mom's illness, I had a difficult time creating these moments of joy. I would have to make a conscious effort to make myself smile and to engage in our daily play. So, joy became watching *Judge Judy* and *The Big Bang Theory* with Mom. Joy was watching her eat her ice cream even though I knew she might suffer a little later. Joy was observing Mom's delight in driving through our old neighborhood and seeing new construction projects. Joy was rocking my head at the same time Mom was patting her hand on the seat cushion while we listened to classic R&B in the car. Joy was seeing her laugh with her friends, even though I knew that sometimes she was not quick enough to understand a joke or to know what they were laughing about. Finding joy in the moments of now is what I sought. Seeing Mom in her purest state of living provided me with those moments of joy. She made me smile. I knew I could bounce back and take on the challenges of the day. I found joy in Jean. Yet the question remained: Could I find joy in the moment as Mom transitioned into the last stage of her life?

Chapter 16

Reframing

You can't go back and change the beginning, but you can
start where you are and change the ending.

Unknown

$\mathcal{I}$f I wanted to provide the best experiences for Mom, I had
to learn to focus on creating the best experiences for myself.
Little did I know the two were connected. I knew that Mom and I
would have richer moments if I consciously tried to rethink how I
would respond to situations I could not control. That was my ulti-
mate desire. Knowing that her days were limited, it was important
for her not to feel my stress or anger. She did not deserve that. She
struggled to be seen and heard, so why would I allow my shadow
to block her from existing in the light? To surrender, I would have
to learn to reframe situations to achieve different outcomes and
I would have to concentrate on rethinking my response in the
moment.

I was very familiar with the concept of reframing. The act of
reframing is a strategy frequently used during leadership coaching.
Executive and leadership coaches use the technique of reframing

or facilitating the client to shift his or her perspective by asking powerful questions. During a podcast created by a dear friend of mine, I discussed the concept of reframing in the experiences of women leaders. We discussed how reframing is used in a women's leadership model I developed based on my research into African American women's leadership experiences in private industry. Black women leaders in private industry told me stories about using reframing to settle conflicts or behaviors used against them. They use reframing to prohibit racism from overshadowing their successes and achievements in the corporate world.

Reframing was historically even used to create a new reality of Black servitude, inferiority, and sexual denigration. Negative situations were reframed into more tolerable ones. The women I interviewed had to flip this negative narrative of subhuman existence to belief in themselves. They had to reframe occurrences of bias against them to rise out of the ashes like phoenixes and create images of strength, resilience, and tenacity to overcome age-old myths of inferiority. They took a negative comment and turned it into an opportunity to demonstrate their ability. They reframed a corporate challenge into a corporate win.

I quickly learned I could apply the concept of reframing to my experience as Mom's primary caregiver. I could shift the value I placed on guidelines I created for her care. Following the same course as the women in my research, I would have to reframe situations regarding Mom's illness as well. For example, reframing could mean learning to choose the right battles to fight or ignoring others' behavior that would not have a direct impact on Mom.

Stories of waiting long periods of time to get assistance was the norm. I held my breath as anxiety flooded my body every time Mom paged for assistance. Often, the staff attributed the wait to understaffing and an overreliance on temporary workers. Even so, there were also times when staff simply ignored my mom. One time, I found her aide downstairs in the lobby laughing and talking with another aide after Mom had pushed the call button several times. He was standing right next to the receptionist's desk. I know my plea to the receptionist to find someone to help Mom and the corresponding look on my face, caused the aide to halt his conversation, quickly jump on the elevator, and tend to Mom's needs.

Another time, Mom and I sat in her room for forty-five minutes waiting for someone to take her to the bathroom. After pushing the button for assistance multiple times, Mom headed for the door to the hallway to find someone to help her. I stopped her, told her to wait, and took the elevator downstairs to let the receptionist know that my mother's aides had not responded to the page. Finally, after a total of fifty minutes of waiting, someone came to assist her. Fortunately, most of the time, Mom's medication was administered in a timely manner, although there were missteps because she couldn't communicate directly with the staff.

I eventually learned that I was limited in how quickly I could turn things around for the benefit of her care. I tried to reframe events and seriously examine dated frames of references and responses I've relied upon most of my life, realizing that hardwired beliefs often keep me living in a kind of paralysis, much like the storied definition of insanity as doing the same thing over and over again and expecting different results. Rather, my mantra became, "If I respond the same way all the time, I will get the same results."

Unfortunately, we sometimes rely on old narratives to interpret the events of the present. Holding onto these outdated narratives can sometimes threaten our well-being. Reframing helped me to restructure the stark and challenging realities of caring for Jean Jordan. Old stories and societal and family norms were no longer useful or relevant, and they created additional fear and guilt in me. Eventually, I embarked on a new path by doing my best to socially construct another reality or a different outcome.

There were times when I had to hold my breath and intentionally tweak my response to a difficult circumstance by hijacking my emotional response to achieve a prefrontal cortex-related response. So, if it took someone a while to take care of Mom's toileting needs, I reminded myself to reframe the situation and identify other possibilities and reactions. Instead of expecting the negative first, I generated another possibility. Maybe the staff was overwhelmed by the amount of work demanded of them. Maybe Mom was not present at one of the musical events simply because she chose not to attend, rather than the staff failing to let her know about the event. In real time, I was learning how to put my emotions in check by exploring other probable causes for actions and mishaps related to her quality of care.

There were times when I wasn't successful in reframing and my emotions hijacked me. During these times, my emotional intelligence plummeted to new lows and I no longer existed in the space of peak performance, self-awareness, and critical self-management. But I knew I could not give up, not only for my sanity but Mom's as well. I knew fighting for a new approach could assist me with surrendering—with letting go. I incorporated rituals in my life to support me in shifting my perspective, with the hopes of leading me to respond in a more positive way when things fell through the cracks. Daily practices helped me to create a structured and disciplined approach to dealing with willful neglect and care for Mom. Adopting new practices provided me with opportunities for self-care. I could not forget about my personal needs.

Mom's illness forced me to continue to unlearn fixed constructions of life that I have held onto for decades and to see that human behavior is not fixed. For example, I thought everyone working in the facilities where she received care was truly committed to doing outstanding work. I was raised to believe that everyone worked hard and strived for excellence. I thought the staff would ensure that Mom was fed and bathed. Yet many times, her food tray was not within arm's reach for her to feed herself. After she was released from the hospital following her stroke, she was served solid food when she should have received pureed food. I presumed information about Mom's health was shared during shift changes, and that aides and nurses taking care of her read her medical chart to glean important facts. But that was not the case. And I thought as well that the staff knew not to wash Mom's dark clothes with her white clothes. I discovered quickly that wasn't the case either—fur balls, discoloration, lint, and missing lingerie—oh my! A few of these examples may appear trite and insignificant, but a daily dose of any one of these failed expectations caused me to descend into the pits of anger and despair.

I would have to change my perspective and tweak my strict views of how things are supposed to be and view them the way they are in the moment, regardless of whether I agreed. The more I gave in to societal and self-imposed boundaries around my thinking, the more I would struggle to live a life of peace, contentment, and gratitude. The more I held onto these thoughts, the more I would only see a fence in front of the house blocking me from entering a new world of ideas, instead of moving to the side of the house where there was no fence at all. It is all about our perspectives, which can change, and how we choose to respond. Both are in our purview of control. I have a long way to go before I will see the opportunity to enter a house of new ideas by altering my perspective, but it is a worthwhile journey. My journey with Mom was worthwhile. A shift in my perspective opened the door for greater understanding and more empathy during those moments of uncertainty and it became easier to move on.

Chapter 17

Forgiveness Is Freedom

Why do you stay in prison when the door is
so wide open.

Rumi

*M*om's illness created a void in my life. Her motherly ways were now affected by her struggle to speak, her desire to walk, and at times, her inability to tap into the nurturing part of her brain.

Mom's illness also tested my ability to forgive. For two and a half years, I faced many situations that engendered emotions and feelings I had never experienced before. Of course, I had been angry before, but my body experienced extreme conditions of unrelenting and uncontrollable rage that were somatic in nature. I would experience vertigo, heart palpitations, and extreme sorrow. Many times, I felt alone with my feelings, which, unsurprisingly, was not new to me. I was accustomed to feeling like an emotional aberration throughout my life. But my inability to forgive proved to be the most self-destructive behavior with the greatest impact on me. I found myself holding onto anger towards everyone because

I felt they were not supporting Mom the way that I thought they should. Looking back on these moments, I discovered that most of the time, it was not about Mom. Rather, it was about me. I was crying out for help in the most destructive ways. Expressing anger was my way of getting attention because I did not know what else to do. I was lost in the wilderness, looking for someone to save me from a void in my life. Mom was normally the person I would go to when I was lost. I did not always agree with her response, but I knew that she would always be there.

I was living the reality of Audre Lorde's observation: "Your silence will not protect you." It was crucial to respond in a different way. I had to learn how to let my close circle of friends and family know my needs, but still understand they would not always respond the way I needed them to respond. The person with whom I shared my challenges may not always have had the emotional intelligence or emotional bandwidth to join in my hurt and pain. However, life is a risk, and choosing how you respond, according to Viktor Frankl, is freeing. The only other option is to let resentment and anger ravage our souls. We can choose.

I waited for someone to voluntarily and intuitively stand in a gap that was wide and deep. What I should have done was ask for help. But I did not know how, so at times I assumed the role of a victim to get attention. Victimhood was not unique to me. Most people have assumed this role at some point in their life.

During a phone conversation, I remember a friend accusing me of acting like a victim. It took me several months to realize he was right. Wasn't I allowed to be a victim at a time in my life when I felt trapped? Are we all so perfect that there aren't times when we do not have the courage to tell our loved ones we need their support? The comment cut deeply in the moment, and it came as Mom lay in her hospital bed next to me. Mom died two weeks after my friend's accusation. It became difficult for me to separate that incident from the need I had for unconditional support. Mom was very ill and approaching the end of life. That was all I could think about. Sadly, it would take months for me to forgive my friend. However, not only did I have to forgive my friend, but I also had to forgive myself for contributing to the exchange. I was not authentic in the relationship. I should have said, "I need you to be by my side." But I did not. I knew that I would have to forgive my friend to appropriately move through my grief and surrender to a new day. The timing of the conversation and the vitriol behind the message made it hard for me to swallow, but there was something for me to learn, even in a conversation with an unhappy outcome.

Throughout my life, I have never had a significant problem forgiving. I was predestined to offload hurt and pain caused by someone else. It was in my DNA. I did not hold onto what someone may have done or said to me that generated hurt at the time. With an extremely sensitive spirit, many times I was the target of teasing and bullying. Especially as a child and teenager, it did not take much to make me cry. Through all the teasing and bullying, I always found it in my heart to forgive. With bottled-up emotions and too proud to ask for help, I created an island only I inhabited during Mom's illness. I isolated myself and closed the door to most people, even family. All I could see at the time was Mom's failing health and the shortcomings of the staff. Unfortunately, a slow descent to a nervous breakdown was not impossible for me. I was traumatized.

Several years ago, I discovered that I am an empath. This illuminated the "why" of my past behaviors that people close to me could not understand. I frequently heard, "Cheryl, you are too sensitive." "Why would you let that bother you?" "Get over it." As I got older, I began to believe that these statements accurately described me. It took years for me to be okay with being me and to recognize the gift of empathy that I use to assist my clients with changes and help them live with purpose. My gift of empathy also served as a guide to forgiveness. And through my empathy, I can see layers of the heart. I listen to others when no one else does. I welcome the whole person, problems and all, not just the part I want to hear.

As a child, I was an easy mark for teasing because of my sensitivities. I soon recognized that some negative behaviors directed towards me were not always about something I did. Many times, the behaviors were a result of someone projecting their personal pain onto me. It took a lot for me to fight back. I weighed a little over sixty pounds and was one of the shortest kids in my class in the sixth grade. I did not have the typical stature associated with toughness and the ability to fight back. With eyes the size of saucers and a body that could easily fit into a girl's size eight, I found myself escaping many moments of ridicule. By the time I was fourteen, I was five feet, eight-and-a-half inches tall, a lanky girl without curves. Boys weren't interested in flirting with me, even though I was fully ready to experience first love.

As I grew taller, my self-esteem grew shorter. The bullying continued, and several times I wondered if anyone would miss me if I were no longer alive. I had a strong need for belonging but was not savvy at navigating all the dynamics and issues associated with the early teenage years. Through all the bullying, it was very easy for me to forgive. Yet years later, I found myself in the same place, but with one change. I was bullying myself by allowing my anger to co-opt my life. My heart was cold as ice. I walked through this time in my life on a tightrope with a fragile spirit.

My friend Nicole always told me I was a heart person longing for acceptance. She would know, as she and I had hours-long conversations during which we dissected and examined our emotional responses to important events in our lives. As my spiritual mentor, Nicole helped me see the beauty of my emotional DNA. She spiritually guided me through some tough times, like when I found out I was pregnant as a single woman.

Nicole knew everything. She could tell you the day I thought I conceived, my original due date, and the date on which I gave birth to my son. She could tell you my fears and my deep concerns about getting pregnant by someone who I did not know was doing drugs. I found safety in our quiet moments of sharing, especially when I needed to unpack boyfriend chronicles. But the most beautiful thing I can say about her is that she helped me to be okay with all my sensitivities and tears. Her life stories became guideposts for where I should or should not venture in my life. We were and still are kindred spirits.

It would take years for me to eventually accept my emotional and sensitive brilliance, linked to my keen intuition. I learned that my empathic abilities allowed me to let go and forgive. Forgiving others and myself became a pathway to personal freedom. The burden of controlling or holding onto any hurt can sever the lifeline to releasing and moving forward.

I learned that it is okay to forgive yourself for being angry and having unrealistic expectations of others during critical times. Not everyone could jump on board and handle Mom's care the way that I did. Someone else could say that I did not do enough. In life, everything is relative. But I created a norm for care. It was either this way or that way, nothing in between. My thinking was grounded as a young child to think life occurred in black or white.

I was taught to believe that Dick, Jane, and Spot were good, but my caramel skin and tightly coiled hair were not. The objective reality did not include me. I did not see myself in commercials, except on a bottle of syrup or on a pancake box. I did not hear about Black Wall Street in Tulsa, Oklahoma, or Durham, North Carolina. I never heard about Harriet Tubman's fight against lynching or the powerful Colored Women's Movement of the late 1800s and early 1900s. Why did I not hear about the Talented Tenth? Or Katherine Johnson? Dorothy Vaughan? Mary Jackson? Each of these women played a major role in the historical launch of John Glenn into orbit. In the same way that I encountered walls of exclusion, I created a similar reality regarding Mom's caregiving. My expectation was that everyone cared for Mom the way I did. My expectations were exclusionary in nature.

It was burdensome not to forgive. It was like an albatross around my neck, permanently affixed to an old story that was no longer relevant. Unforgiveness pushed me further into a valley where the possibilities of living a fruitful life were impossible to see because I was focusing on the ground. What I saw influenced my ability to take steps forward and narrowed my view of what was waiting for me to rise. During moments when I was stuck viewing the ground, I began to look for things to confirm my feelings, which agreed with my actions, and that caused me to look in a single direction. It felt impossible to see a 360-degree view of the circumstances of Mom's care.

My inability to forgive not only affected me but also negatively invaded the well-being of others in my circle of family and friends. The combination of my inability to forgive and my corresponding anger could destroy the family's positive core—one consisting of love and laughter. I had to let go, be free, and examine my beliefs. Like my mother fighting for her life in the ICU, I knew I could be reborn or somehow reverse the process of an emotional death. I knew there was more for me to do in this lifetime, so I had to work on breaking the stronghold of anger and forgive to be free.

Chapter 18

The Shine of Love

*In all the world there is no heart for me like yours. In all
the world there is no love for you like mine.*

Maya Angelou

On numerous occasions, Mom used to remind me that I
would be alright amidst challenging times. Because I was not
always ready to hear her direct and sharp commentary, her words
left me a little angry. Even so, they also provided me with fruitful
food for thought. I felt safe knowing she was on my side. She was
a diehard supporter who helped me to unravel and explore the
negative energy that often haunted my soul. Jean helped me pick
up the pieces and forge ahead with a fighting spirit that could beat
any foe.

I believe that with God's help our mothers breathe life into
our bodies, and although one day they will certainly die, their love
is magical and enduring. Their love remains peacefully by our
sides even after death, with the power to correct destructive family conflict, soothe broken hearts, and help us stand for change.
A mother's love is weather, water, and fireproof. A mother's love

knows no boundaries and envelops our total being. My mother's love was not restricted by boundaries.

During the sixty-three years of our life on earth with one another, Mom frequently reminded me that I was an awesome daughter, although I believe I could have done more for her. She would say how proud she was of her children and grandchildren. Always transparent and direct, I knew where I stood in her eyes, even in times of mother-daughter chaos and disagreement. However, during moments of serious discord, I never questioned her love for me or my three brothers.

Reflecting on the force of her love, I became sad and remorseful because of the way I treated her, especially when I was a teenager. Even now, I continue to apologize for my chaotic, emotional, and childlike behaviors and wish I could take all of them back. The reality is that I was just a kid, but fragments of the remorse and guilt remain with me today. As a mature woman with similar experiences to Mom's, I am now humbled by her life. I bow down to her tenacity and the legacy of love she left for us to pass on to our children. I embrace her history and life experiences with tender care and homage. I see her light and shine of love as a mother. She never turned her back on me, even when I challenged her every word. Mom was my lifeline to internal beauty as a woman who passed on her shine to me so that I could pass it on to my son.

My caregiving experiences led me up and down a roller coaster of gratitude. Spending moments with Mom ignited a passion of thankfulness. Charting this new course, I not only saw the darkness associated with my caregiving experiences but the tenderness of Mom. I held onto expressions of *mojuba*, an Afro-Cuban religious concept with roots in Yoruba Nigerian culture, one associated with the act of thanking and honoring ancestors. Mom's illness created thankfulness and gratitude in my heart. I was grateful for her unconditional love for me and my brothers. I was grateful for the past, and for the present moments I could spend with her. In those moments of gratefulness, I realized that she was a major force in my life. I recognized that many of my accomplishments were because of her quietly pushing me to the edge, encouraging me not to be afraid as I leaped into the unknown.

About a dozen years before Mom passed away, she encouraged me to enroll in a doctoral program. She knew I had the opportunity to enroll in a doctoral program shortly after receiving my masters in 1989 with the support of a scholarship offered to me at the University of Cincinnati. As a single parent with a nine-year-old son, my priority was finding employment at the time. I declined the offer from the university ombudsman's office without hesitation or regret. Iman was my priority. Enriching his life was my focus. Mom replied, "I would like to see you receive your doctorate before I leave this earth." Her words stayed with me.

With her desire and a push from two friends, I eventually enrolled in a program that changed my life. In 1989, I found employment after completing my master's degree. Financially underwater, I could not even afford a suit for my interview. Mom graciously stepped in and purchased a navy-blue interview suit for me, which helped me land the job of my dreams at the time. *Mojuba*! Thank you, Jean Jordan, for being a role model of love and compassion. You taught me how to show love and support. Thank you for inserting yourself into an equation leading to quick action and results—especially because I was at a loss for what steps to take next and totally exhausted from participating in a demanding program while I looked after Iman's every need.

Mom's love for me was infinite and undaunted by the inevitable transitions in the circle of life. At least that had been my experience. Even months after her passing, I could still feel the force of her love. It surrounded me and reminded me of the intensity and energy of caring. Her loyalty and love made me realize if everyone on this earth could care about each other as deeply as she cared about me and the rest of her family, we could tear down the walls of intolerance, xenophobia, and hatred in this world. The power of Mom's love convinced me to continue to take baby steps toward internalizing the energy emanating from the shine of her love. Caring for her opened my eyes to the powerhouse she was. She propelled me toward greatness even when I doubted myself.

Just like Jean Jordan, everyone can leave a legacy of love if we embrace our true nature as compassionate, caring, and communal beings. I believe we were created and destined to take care of each other, feed the human spirit, and improve the human condition. The shine of this legacy of love opens our hearts, soothes our pain, and creates unconditional love and acceptance for each other. We learn to walk a path of non-judgment and vulnerability when faced with the shine of love, and we reflect that love to others in our circle of experience.

The shine of love blinds our fears, which can sometimes lead to hatred. Our brains are wired for survival. When our survival is threatened, we fight or flee out of fear. Hatred is a manifestation of fear. Hatred makes it possible for us to destroy and alienate the groups of people who threaten our survival. With love, our perspectives change. We begin to see that fear of another human being is not warranted because we can see the love and concern in them. I am convinced that we all crave and need the benefits derived from the shine of love. Unfortunately, our deepest fears are grounded in the insecurity of our survival. Negative stimuli from multiple media platforms every day invade our lives, keeping us stuck in a fearful state of mind.

At a workshop several years ago, I remember a facilitator asking each participant to stand and identify his or her biggest fear in the workplace. Before the exercise began, I saw the look of pain on other participants' faces about publicly sharing their fears. This is a feeling that is common when working in environments where the smartest and most fearless are revered. We are afraid to share our fears because we are afraid of being discovered as not good enough—as intruders or impostors. As all two dozen of us sat there, believing that we did not belong, a team member courageously entered a space of vulnerability in a conference room filled with anxiety. Slowly and sometimes painfully, each employee stood up and shared her or his fear of not being smart enough, or good enough—all the "not enough" that has haunted humanity since the dawn of time.

After hearing a variety of fears from the team, the facilitator summarized the point of the exercise with a simple but prophetic response that continues to resonate with me even today. "Fear creates all dysfunction in organizations." Silence followed her words. No one said a word. She nailed what I had been searching to understand in one very simple statement. Her comment helped me to look at negative issues and problems between employees differently. Most of the time, conflicts arose from employees' livelihoods being threatened. Amazingly, the exercise inspired rich discussion among the team, something that was necessary to create a more collaborative team.

However, even after learning these insights, some team members still walked away from the exercise concerned about what others were thinking about them. Unveiling their fears left them feeling vulnerable and open to criticism, casting doubt on how they perceived their professional identity.

In our minds, we all question who we are by comparing ourselves to a point on a continuum representing the norm. We all seek, as Luther Vandross sings, "the glow of love," the glow of knowing that we are enough. We compare ourselves to professional colleagues, family, friends, and even people we do not know. What we seek is survival based, and unfortunately, this quest for affection is not limited to the workplace. We can also crave the same approval, unconditional affiliation, and love at home every evening.

Shortly after moving to Atlanta, my husband at the time, brother, and I were driving on a major street in midtown Atlanta one evening. We noticed a man lying in the street near the curb. There was a lot of traffic, and I was concerned about his safety. Clearly, we could see that he had had too much to drink and was likely homeless. Despite resistance from my husband about stopping, my brother and I pulled the car over, jumped out, and ran to his aid. Our instincts and actions to help this man were natural, and I was stunned by my husband's stubbornness to get out of the car. Only a couple of months into the marriage, I could see that our hearts were not equally yoked. This is not to say that love was not inside of him, but I wondered what prevented him from wanting to help a person in such great need. As a child and teenager, I witnessed feats of bravery from both my parents. Neither of them turned their backs on anyone in crisis mode. The gene of compassion was passed down to me and the rest of my siblings. The lack of compassion shown by my husband's behavior was foreign and disturbing. Even to this day, I will always wonder what dimmed his shine.

Chapter 19

A Love Story

Good night, princess.

Jean Jordan

$\mathcal{M}$y journey as a caregiver is also a story of love between a mother and daughter. I realized during Mom's illness that loving relationships are often taken for granted. Relationships are full of habitual behaviors, automatic responses, and uninformed assumptions. We glide through our relationships with loved ones, never stopping to revel in or demonstrate the love we have for each other. Loving gestures are reserved for birthdays, Mother's and Father's Day, and other holidays. We show our love through the gifts we purchase and the Easter outfits we buy for our kids. Although love may be deeply ingrained in the relationship, it may not be expressed through words or moments of intimate sharing.

A chapter of a new love story with Mom began the moment she reached out to me while she was in intensive care. During that moment, I knew there was no going back to old stories, and to moments of pain we had created for each other over the years. I realized in our relationship how tender moments of intimacy can ground a relationship in authenticity and confidence and trust in one another. Even if Mom snarled at me, I quickly transitioned from anger to appreciation. Even if she pushed my hand away, I emotionally jumped from feelings of hurt to humor. Even if I made her angry, I knew that she was waiting at the door for me. Our story was a story of unconditional love.

I wish that I could say that I did not let old stories and misunderstandings from previous years to cloud my judgment and interfere with our time together. But I did. I beat the hell out of conflicts or misunderstandings that happened between us when I was a child. At the time of our altercations, I did not understand the depth of my own sensitivities. You could say *boo* to me, and I would cry. I wore my feelings on my sleeve.

After her stroke, I greeted my mother with a kiss every day I saw her. Without fail, I told her how much I loved her. I tended to her sadness with warm embraces. My love for Mom grew daily as I held her hand tightly. I reminded her that she was the best mother in the whole wide world. Our relationship evolved and became stronger every day even though sometimes she was limited in her ability to understand what was going on. And in the moment, I did not always grasp how the kinetic force of being close to someone every day, even when things were not always pleasant, could create a stronger bond between two people.

I remember experiencing our bond as mother and daughter during an old-fashioned school prom organized by the long-term care facility for the residents. Mom refused to get dressed up in formal attire reminiscent of the 1950s and 1960s. Although she could not express that it seemed hokey to her, I knew her reasons. How she presented herself to the world was always important.

The first stop of the long-awaited event included a photographer ready to take a picture of us in front of a background of stars dangling from the ceiling. We were transported back in time as we entered the dining room that had been transformed into a ballroom, helping residents imagine that they were once again at the prom. We were greeted by soft music playing from a time when crooners sang "Up on the Roof" in perfect harmony and Etta James bellowed "At Last" with her sultry, raspy, contralto voice. The DJ even played a few tunes by Frank Sinatra. During their youth, the women residents had likely worn flowing gowns and gloves up to their elbows, so it was a beautiful memory to see them dressed up again in organza and chiffon evening gowns purchased off the racks of secondhand and consignment shops or rescued from a trunk in the attic. They were women from a generation where rhinestones and pearls bedazzled and framed their necks and ears and when women knew that dressing modestly was required. A few of the residents even wore tiaras.

Mom smiled as we sat on the sidelines observing the enthusiasm and tender moments exchanged between attendees who were experiencing magic from the past. The excitement in the room floated from wheelchair to wheelchair, from corsage to corsage, and from boutonniere to boutonniere. I could envision residents remembering their youth and dancing with their first loves. Mom sat quietly, trying to concentrate on everything she observed in the room.

The culminating event was the announcement of the prom king and queen. Both winners were in their nineties and suffered from dementia, but they could still stand. They held each other closely as they danced to a ballad from the past. It was one of the most enchanting moments I have experienced in my life. I could tell that Mom's sentiment matched mine. She began to weep uncontrollably, and I understood what prompted her tears. She felt the love as well. And as she wept, *I* began to cry. I knew that she was thinking about the love she had for Dad and the times they held each other closely. She knew those times were no longer possible. They were now a part of history. I held her hand and wiped her tears. The moment became unbearable for her, so we decided to leave. In the moment of both of us crying together, our love for each other was further sealed and strengthened even without me realizing it.

Our moments of bonding continued to strengthen during exciting moments. One sunny winter afternoon, once Mom was strong enough to sit up on her own for long periods of time, she rode with me to pick up her sister from the airport. I could sense her excitement as the aides transferred her from her wheelchair into the car. I decided to take the scenic route because I knew it would motivate her to fight for her health. She sat stately and looking dignified on the passenger side, pointing at buildings and homes she remembered. In some instances, she responded with a "Wow!" The things she had taken for granted as she drove by on her way to work for thirty years were like a brand-new world for her. No longer confined to a building, she could experience a different scene. I joined her excitement as we drove through the city known for its seven hills and beautiful views of the Ohio Valley. We crossed the Brent Spence Bridge, spanning the Ohio River, to get to the Cincinnati airport that, surprising to many, is in northern Kentucky. Once in Kentucky, we stopped at a gas station and loaded up on all sorts of junk food and pop. We were in paradise as our mother and daughter bond grew while we took turns digging into the bag of Grippo potato chips.

It was moments like these over the two-and-a-half years of her illness that brought us ever closer together. It was moments like these that reminded me that she was my first love and provider. She heard my cries during the most extreme moments in my life and taught me how to be a beautiful and powerful Black woman and a responsible mother to my son. She was more than a role model mother to me. She was a major character in one of the greatest love stories of my life.

Chapter 20

A Journey of Change

The cave you fear to enter holds the treasure you seek.

Joseph Campbell

Joseph Campbell researched ancient mythologies from all over the world. A common theme emerging from his research is the archetype he calls the "Hero's Journey." All of us have experienced this journey at some point in our lives. Rebecca Chan Allen, the author of *Guiding Change Journeys,* describes the journey of change as initially existing in a status quo state of being, either accepting mediocrity or sameness or lacking originality and creativity in our lived experiences. Then, with or without warning, a call for change interrupts the inertia, causing us to jump into an abyss of uncertainty, fear, and loss of control. We encounter trials and tribulations during the journey, not knowing that we must first fight the serpents of the sea and the cyclops in hidden caverns, meet our mentors to help us sort it out, or tread a territorial maze of dead ends before we discover the golden fleece. Along the way, we encounter something like a magic elixir that heals us and heals the world and society around us as well.

As the journey continues, we reconcile what was with what is. Although this stage of the journey may feel chaotic and tumultuous, something powerful is stirring underneath, if only we allow the powerful forces of nature to guide us along the way. This phase requires resilience. Our responses and movement must be grounded in the faith of knowing that one day we will make it to the top of the mountain and champion a new day. Reflecting on the journey, new learning is illuminated, but sometimes we do not take the time to investigate where we are and how to apply this new knowledge in our lives.

Difficult transitions can show us who we are, what is important, and how we figure out a way to survive. As I embarked on a similar journey with my mother, I wondered what this new experience would teach me. Would I walk away with nuggets of gold or elevated wisdom? Or would the magic elixir allude me and would I find myself at the end of the journey permanently broken and lost?

In my story, there was new knowledge and wisdom for me to receive. During my journey, I learned the true value of patience and humility. I had to examine my responses to everyone that was in my mother's circle of relationships. Demonstrating patience proved to be a difficult feat. There were moments when I became enraged when individual actions did not meet my expectations. I knew if I continued to challenge the beliefs of others that were contrary to mine, I would fail. If I was going to get to the other side of this journey, I would have to pick my battles and my method of warfare. Aggressive behavior was seldom the right approach. Making others feel guilty for not meeting my expectations for taking care of Mom was a recipe for disaster. Making others feel guilty was my cry for help. It was my SOS call. But it did not work. On the contrary, it was destructive to place guilt on others. It caused discord. But I also learned that the desperate fight for my life and well-being was my right and was nothing to be ashamed of. I had to meet myself where I was at the time and acknowledge that my intentions were not to hurt anyone during the fight.

If I had the opportunity to step into my past, I am not sure if I would have changed my approach to Mom's care. I could have engaged in more social activities to take my mind off what was going on. In retrospect, switching from the tactic of guilt trolling to self-disclosing my pain and fear with my family and friends may have reduced the amount of stress I endured as well. I complained about the support I was not getting and did not share the emotional support I needed.

I also learned that patience grants us the space to rest in our thoughts and to see other possibilities. Demonstrating patience towards my mom helped me to see her happiness as she initiated the smallest acts of independence, like washing the parts of her body that she could reach, brushing her teeth, or directing me to go home in the evenings when she needed her space. A little patience can remove the barriers of misunderstanding during critical conversations and change. I needed to hear the voices of my ancestors, remember their fight to survive, and experience *Sankofa* moments that were in the act of engaging myself in retrieving and learning from the past. I asked Mother Martha, my grandmother who died many years ago, "How did you respond when you experienced trauma or saw someone in pain?" I called on my deceased grandmother, Addie Pearl, to show me how to have a gentle and kind spirit when I was angry. I heard Grand Daddy play the harmonica and speak *Kouri-Vini*, a Louisiana Creole language, and this made me smile as if I were still a child.

But there were times when it was difficult to be patient. Counting to ten did not help. And when I tried to walk away, I immediately circled back to a place of conflict as I confronted the issue. I found that it was difficult to juggle patience with outright neglect regarding Mom's care. Occasionally, I was led to extreme states of confrontation.

One day I found Mom still in bed and soaked in urine at 11:00 a.m. When I entered her room, Mom saw the shocked look on my face and shrugged her shoulders as if to say, "I do not know what is going on." We both tore off her overnight pad. It was so soaked that it felt like it weighed a couple of pounds, a sign that she had not been switched out before the shift change at 7:00 a.m. No longer grounded in logic, I held the pad between my thumb and index finger, walked out of Mom's room, and marched down the hallway with the pad dangling, ignoring the troubled looks of other residents and staff along the way. I entered the charge nurse's office, startling her while she sat at her computer. She was in shock. Holding the pad in full view of her, I commented aggressively, "This is unacceptable!" She was at a loss for words for a few seconds before asking me what had happened. She was one of the few nurses that did not discount or diminish my actions. She was concerned about Mom's care. Her quick response was to immediately escalate the incident to the nursing home director, who profusely apologized to Mom and me. Yet, the lack of proper care within this long-term care facility was ingrained in its culture.

These circumstances tested my patience, fueled my fight, and led me to challenge the owner of the nursing home on several occasions. Unfortunately, after this incident things regarding Mom's care only changed for a few days. Some level of neglect continued. At some point, my family and I decided it was time to move her to another facility.

The charge nurse had a stroke several weeks later. She was only in her late forties. Curiously, I wondered if the stress of working at a facility that is designed to be ineffective could have caused her unfortunate illness. Working in an industry that is known for paying low wages and having frequent staffing shortages can create an environment in which the staff is always running behind.

Pain without a release valve can create substantial internal pressure. Sometimes, the release valve that we seek to relieve the pain is unhealthy and destructive. However, the release valve can also direct our path to wholeness and an understanding of why the pain existed in the first place. I experienced a great deal of pain while caregiving. Some of the pain was self-induced; I did not know how to manage my emotional state of being.

Over forty years ago, when Dad was in intensive care for three months and tied to his bed because of experiencing alcohol withdrawal, Mom was there to help ease my pain. When Dad entered the hospital again a year later and died within three days of his admission for the same addiction problem, Mom was there to help ease my pain. When I had to start my life over again as a twenty-year-old without Dad's laughter, Mom was there to help ease my pain.

Forty-three years later, things were different. Mom was dealing with her own pain and was no longer available to dull the pain I was experiencing, which I carried for three years without release. Yes, there were a few family members and friends who sometimes took care of me. My son took care of me from the West Coast, his grandmother in New Jersey checked on me, and my brother in Washington, DC, was armed with love and caring for me. But I couldn't find a permanent escape route for my pain. I was stuck on a roller coaster ride of life and had to hold tight to the handlebars to survive. Although I had some support, I was at a loss for how to support myself without taking attention away from Mom. Unfortunately, this pain found fertile ground and rooted in my body. I would later suffer from the physical manifestations of unreleased hurt and sorrow. Lacking a pressure valve would leave uncurable cracks in my soul.

Diamonds and crystals can withstand tremendous pressure, but our souls can cave under the unrelenting pressures of life if we do not have avenues of support. Our personal shine can lose its brilliance. Our mental well-being struggles for a place of peace and then one day we find ourselves close to having a mental breakdown. That was me. Again, I did not know how to let my family know what I really needed to feel safe and supported. I expected everyone to know what to do to support me.

Growing up and as an adult, I remember Mom saying to me on numerous occasions, "Cheryl, that is how you would do it, but everyone is not like you." My mom taught me one of the hardest lessons for me to learn. Even to this day, it is a constant battle for me to let go of projecting my personal expectations onto others. Mom encouraged me not to judge people for not responding or showing up the way I think they should have. You never know what was going on in their lives.

Life is funny in that way. Pain and hurt can often be our greatest teachers. When they no longer blot out our mental, emotional, and physical well-being and we intentionally get quiet and reflect on what's occurred, the lesson is waiting to be discovered. It is vital to seek the lesson with vigilance, curiosity, objectivity, and with an open heart. Creating a sacred place for healing is critical to hearing what life whispers.

Joseph Campbell writes, "Your sacred space is where you can find yourself over and over again." Uncovering life lessons also requires focused action and attention. Life lessons may not always fall from the heavens or show up on a highway billboard. Soren Kierkegaard, a Danish philosopher, theologian, social critic, and existentialist observed, "Life can only be understood backwards; but it must be lived forwards." So, the culminating event of the hero's journey is to use the learning for change and community building, for personal evolution and actualization, and for sharing and forwarding wisdom to help others. I wrote the following during one of my journaling sessions while working on my doctoral research several years ago. It relates to my hero's journey as a caregiver:

I always knew that there was something that needed to blossom within. Curiosity provoked learning and seeing with a third eye... my soul...my heart...my mind is altered...transformed by stories of yesterday and future visions. Living in a half-lit room of darkness, but now in a half-lit room of light. Seeing the hearts and hearing the words of others, I now see a new me that always existed. I exhale... rejuvenated...and ready to make a difference.

Chapter 21

Waking Up

That even as we grieved, we grew. That even as we hurt, we hoped.

Amanda Gorman

As I seek personal understanding and growth, it would be irresponsible of me not to address my identity as a Black woman with my many insecurities and how that identity informed my experience as a caregiver. My personal research on Black women in leadership positions and working in corporations highlighted the impact of multiple identities converging and informing their lived experiences. The intersectionality of these identities fueled dangerous stereotypes and generalities. It also framed a false image of what I should be as a Black woman.

A prominent idea at the core of these stereotypes and generalities is the ideology of femininity associated with Victorian culture. One stereotype is the mythical Mammy who is the opposite of fragile White femininity. The Mammy is a happy-go-lucky consummate caregiver residing in the master's house. The image of Black women as the non-threatening caregiver continues to exist in contemporary times and so does the perpetual story of the strong Black woman, who is so strong and nurturing that she neglects her own needs.

I am that strong Black woman, and I know so many other Black women who attempt to live this stereotype, even to their own detriment. My automatic response is to nurture, ease the pain, and uplift people regardless of their race, ethnicity, gender, sexual orientation, or identity. I lived as a strong Black woman throughout the two and a half years I spent with Mom.

These stereotypes are still alive. Caricatures of these stereotypes thrive in commercials, social media, movies, and books, informing Black women's beliefs about how they should show up in the world very early in their childhoods. I bought into these beliefs. I walked around with a heavy load filled with so many empty promises for my self-care while caring for Mom. I am not promoting the notion that caring for a loved one is not important and should not require steadfast attention. I am saying that I should have noticed that I was trying to be something that was impossible for me to be. Although I was familiar with these myths, I ignored what I knew to be true.

I lost Mom during this journey of care, but I gained wisdom and knowledge about myself. Although I almost crumbled from seeking an unrealistic outcome and was angry and weary, I grew internally. The ride was not in vain. As we analyze the sequence of our sojourns in life, we will experience a variety of emotions and feelings associated with the jump into new territory. A self-care journey was new territory for me. This ride of a lifetime taught me that in the heat of change, we can fight to peel away layers of pain and fear, we may doubt ourselves, and we may not see the glimmer of hope or new possibilities waiting to be discovered. I am learning to trust the process and permit myself to be human. I want to discover glimmers of hope and new possibilities.

As Mom's mortality was revealed to me, it became even more obvious that the myth of living forever and fighting aging is ingrained in our society. We do whatever we can to smooth the wrinkles, color the gray, and chemically enhance our withering eyebrows so we can hold onto our fleeting youth. I have tried to stave the process of aging, but every time I look in the mirror, I can see the tracks of fine lines searching for new territory into which to expand. I can no longer fool myself. Aging gracefully and with dignity is slowly becoming my motto.

Even after Mom succumbed to a stroke at the age of eighty-two, she was still as beautiful as ever. She was regal. She showed me that there is something powerful about aging. She showed me that you can continue to expect dignity and respect, even when your voice has been silenced, and you have lived for eight decades. She showed me that driving through the city on a sunny day and being inspired by old memories and creating new memories are precious moments. Mom did not let her stroke stop her from venturing outside to watch people and animals and observe the infamous ducks on the property. She was still learning, and she proved that you cannot grow old without learning. Learning in life is like putting baking powder in a pound cake to make it rise. Learning is a leavening agent to help us rise to our greatest heights and to imagine something better for our lives and for society.

Through meditation, I awakened to myriad negative and destructive thoughts trying to take up permanent residence in my mind. Meditation gave me the space to shore up my energy to effectively get through the day. I started with Sarah Blondin, a Canadian whose pre-recorded meditations took me through a journey of loving kindness and self-reverence. Her meditations anchored my soul. The ritual of sitting on the mat every morning illuminated the power of presence. Visits to parks surrounding the area where I lived became even more magical than before. Walking a quarter of a mile to the nearest park was an adventure, not just a walk to rev up my cardio anymore. I asked myself: How often do we break the cycle of habits to experience something fresh and new in our lives? I awakened to how important it was for me to have park encounters, to be close to nature, and to imagine what history existed behind the walls of each house I passed by on my way to the park. Walking through the neighborhood, I saw aspects of the surrounding community that I had never noticed before, although I had known this community for many years before I moved to Atlanta.

One autumn morning about a year before Mom passed, my son and I walked down a street that was new to me in the neighborhood. Iman had flown in from the West Coast to check on Memaw and me. Lined with a canopy of old oak and walnut trees and beautiful old homes from the 1940s, I noticed an older gentleman blowing leaves in his yard. My son and I greeted him as we walked by. He was wearing goggles and a mask over his nose and mouth, so it was very difficult to see his face. But even though most of his face was hidden, there was something familiar about him. He acknowledged us with a nod as we briskly walked by. After we had walked on, I realized that the familiar feeling I had was not a fantasy, but real. I quickly turned around to catch a quick glance at him again, and there he was, standing proud as I remember him from fifty-five years ago, looking at me as if he were waiting for me to turn back around. He then gave me a wave as if he were in a homecoming parade, confirming, Yes, I am someone you know.

I waved back, chuckling to my son that we had just walked by my fifth and sixth-grade physical education teacher, who happened to be one of the first Black teachers I had ever had. This teacher's presence was huge and overpowering for me as a child. He symbolized what I could become in my life regardless of the color of my skin. He made achievement and success believable for me, although it would take years for me to recognize my own unique brilliance and shine. Now, he was retired and a legendary administrator in the Cincinnati public school system. I encountered him a second time and we had the opportunity to reintroduce ourselves to each other and catch up, and for him to lend any support he could to help me with my executive coaching and leadership development business.

Through my journey with Mom, I awakened to the power of unconditional love. Many times, Mom's illness caused her to be aggressive with me, but through it all, my soul only saw a loved one in distress. I could only see how much Mom meant to me. I awakened to how much I loved her and realized she was a source of strength for me before she became ill, and she remained a source of strength after her stroke. I regretted not always giving her the accolades she should have received while she was well. I wished I could replay every argument I had with her and take back every rebellious thing I ever said to her.

I awakened to the degree we can take people who are near and dear to us for granted. Many times, I took Mom for granted. I thought she would always be there. And when she wanted to have a conversation about the inevitability of her mortality, I did not want to hear what she had to say. I wished I would have cherished those precious moments more. I would have asked her more about her life story. I wish I would have asked about the love between her and my father. What was their first date like? When did she realize she was in love with him? When was their first kiss? And where were they? As she made decisions about her memorial services, I could have asked her more about her life before me. But I didn't.

I awakened to my sadness about not creating millions of opportunities to make Mom smile over the years because I held onto pettiness. I fought the change and new information that was meant for me to evolve as a human being. It was easier for me to fight the temptation of imagining something different for my life. Resting in the folds of the norm and even the pain sometimes was easier. I realized that awakening is hard work and demands attention.

I awakened to all these thoughts, constructions, and actions over the course of Mom's illness. The more we were together, the more I could feel our heart connection. The more we were together, the more I realized that her hands were bound by the unfortunate wrappings of a dysfunctional marriage. So how could she be emotionally available for me? Sitting together outside of the assisted living facility, I recognized that all the mess from the past did not matter anymore. Sitting by her side and holding her beautiful hands was enough for me. She was my queen in shining armor and a crown to match, my angel, my *Oshun*, walking in Big Mamma's and Addie Pearl's shine of love.

I discovered, again and again, that the transgressions of the past do not always have to control the present and future moments. I was at liberty to rise above discord and misunderstandings and to believe in a God that gives us all not only a second chance but multiple chances to forgive and accept each other's responses to the conditions and symptoms of just being human. We must acknowledge that we are connected to a larger, all-consuming universe and world with people trying to live their bliss as they fight for survival. Through it all, I felt the connection, saw the bliss, and fought to survive so that I could be there and offer love to Jean Jordan.

If you hear me as I write these words, Jean Jordan, I am grateful. I am grateful for those moments of silence holding your hand. I'm grateful for those moments sitting in the sunshine with you, even though you were bound to your wheelchair. Seeing life reflected in your eyes, I am grateful for the unconditional love that I knew was infinite and lasting. I'm grateful for seeing you and your heart and finally recognizing the richness in your soul. These are the things I have awakened to. These are the things that give me hope and belief in love and forgiveness. I am grateful for the moments of anger we had with each other because they showed the depth of our love. Neither one of us could walk away from each other if we tried. We knew that we both needed each other in so many ways. We would forever be connected to each other through love. I am forever grateful, Mom. Your love energy will never die.

Mom's first cruise—circa 1985

Chapter 22

The Descent

*What we once enjoyed and deeply loved we can never
lose, for all that we love deeply becomes part of us.*

Helen Keller

Who made me the savior of life? I could not control my
Mom's destiny or life's inevitable and universal realities.
I fought to abandon the illogical thoughts that drive my actions,
creating more anxiety for me, my family, and my mother. I could
not resist nature or death. Mom is in the sigh of God's love. She
floats on the breath of light, reminding us how to love. She taught
our family how to come together, encourage, and lift one another.
She compelled us to work through dated family feuds and petty
fights that overshadow the freedom that comes from forgiveness.

Eventually, my mother would no longer play this role, and several months prior to her death I found myself in a state of denial
about her dying. Mom began to decline early in 2018. The decline
was noticeable following a January hospital stay and rehabilitation. There were incremental signs of her decreased vitality; she
was sleeping more but refused to stay in her bed during the night.

A couple of times she pulled herself up, then fell onto the floor. At our request, the staff kept her guardrails up and surrounded her bed with cushions at night. She continued to fall from her bed. She also fell out of her wheelchair several times, most often while napping. Mom was normally very alert in the dining room during meals, but now sitting in the dining room, she would leave her meal untouched and would fall asleep in her wheelchair. She struggled to chew her food or aim her fork towards her mouth.

Looking back at photos, I can see the emptiness and hollowness in her eyes. All the warning signs that Mom was traveling the road to her final destination were there. Unfortunately, I was not prepared. Sometimes I believed that Mom would be here with me and the rest of the family forever, even as she aged. She always managed to bounce back from sickness and challenge of every kind. Surely she would win this battle.

I remember the first time I thought I lost my Mom. I was only five years old. Where was I? Where was Mom? When was she coming back to tuck me in bed and call me princess? I wanted to be with her. I cannot remember every detail of how I ended up at my aunt's house, but I do remember how frightened I was at this unfamiliar and, in my mind, dark place with my brothers and cousins. In reality, Mom had left us for a couple of weeks. She was somewhere in California hoping to mend her broken heart because of the many crises in her relationship with my father. Dad was an extremely sensitive man with a gentle soul and a heart of gold, although his life was haunted by his negative thoughts about himself and his place in the world. He was an empath who had a difficult time managing life in a healthy way. He felt the hurt and pain of others and had a hard time accepting the racism he faced as a classical and jazz guitarist, and surely some of his behaviors were coping mechanisms to help him survive. Mom was just tired, I suppose.

It's startling how childhood memories can continue to haunt you. Sixty years after my mother's brief trip to California, my heart still aches from what I thought was abandonment, but what was simply time for Mom to take a breath and regain her mental and emotional strength. I do not remember when she came back, but I could feel in my body the transition from fear to comfort. Suddenly, I was safe again. We were in the kitchen sitting at the dinner table together once more. She was back, and I was no longer afraid.

There would be more times when I felt like I was losing Mom, but with a strong will, she always fought back. She rebounded after bypass surgery. She bounced back after a serious bout of pancreatitis. She fought for her life as her blood pressure dropped dangerously low after having an angioplasty.

I remember one day, a few weeks before Mom departed this life, I saw surrender in her eyes as we sat outside in the sunshine. Just a short time earlier, we had combed through her closet to reduce some of the clutter and to decide what clothing to give away and what to keep. This delicate and time-consuming task also included her trying on every summer hat that she owned. After marveling at the number of hats she had and deciding which ones she wanted to give away, we both selected one of her hats to wear as we ventured outside for an afternoon stroll. We were the talk of the elevator. We smiled as other residents and family members commented on our wide-brimmed straw chapeaux. I loved to see Mom smile because it meant she was happy again, even if it was just for a short time. After a period of silence sitting outside next to the flower bed, Mom looked into my eyes and began to shake her head from side to side, with a stare engulfed in sadness and strength at the same time. I understood her message and buried my head in her lap, sobbing. I knew what she was conveying. I could read and feel her thoughts: I am tired, and I am dying. She took this brief time in the sunshine to let me know that she had accepted her mortality. But I had not, and I would not until several days before she took her last breath.

It was a strange feeling. Although I knew my mother was not going to live forever, I never thought I would witness her motor skills diminish. Yet, two and a half years after her stroke, her hands began to involuntarily shake. She had a difficult time using her left hand to feed herself, and her right hand and arm were paralyzed from her stroke. Up until a few months before, she continued to fight to take care of herself, even when she did not have the manual dexterity to complete the simplest task. I sometimes wonder if the process of my mother's decline occurred slowly to help prepare me for her transition. There were times when I subconsciously ignored the signs of her withered spirit. Her sunken eyes, her pale complexion. I am sure I was in denial, but she was not. I remember her telling me a story about one of her patients when I was a young adult. She believed he willed himself to death. Someone close to him had just passed away and he felt he had nothing to live for. She said, "Cheryl, he was not that ill. I believe you can will yourself to die. He wanted to die, so he did."

I did not know what to expect when I entered Mom's room each day. Would she be angry, sad, or cheerfully waiting for me to take her outside? Was she tired, beat down and ready to die, or fighting for life so she could see my niece, Kaia, grow into womanhood? Was she fighting for her life so she could see her great grandchildren? Did she ever lose hope? And if she did, at what point did that occur? She believed she would have a new body in her second life, so perhaps that lovely certainty moved her closer to her God.

A few days before I was scheduled to travel to Mexico, Mom was not doing well. She had another UTI; her face was worn and sallow, her eyes sunken. She didn't fight the short trip from the assisted living facility across the street to the hospital. I thought perhaps we would see the forty loose geese that had become an important form of entertainment for Mom. During our daily walks we looked for the flock of geese she had come to love. We clearly noted how they cared and watched out for each other. We knew who the guardian of the flock was, and that we dare not get too close, especially to the goslings.

With support from her friend Tess, we arrived at the hospital. Mom cried when she heard the doctor say she would need to stay there a couple of days. Emotionally spent from two and a half years of chronic infections, gout, atrial fibrillation episodes, diabetic spikes, neuropathic pain, and many other medical challenges, she was tired.

With a UTI and an infected leg because of severe edema, my brother and I made the decision to keep her at the hospital for comfort. The main goal was to avoid sepsis, and to reduce the pain she was feeling because of cellulitis and a potential blood clot. For a minute, I thought about how trying to keep a loved one alive when all the odds are against her can be a perilous journey and an endless cycle of anger, grief, fear, and uncertainty, but I quickly switched my attention to the comments from the hospice nurse: "the hospice can attend to the infection in her leg." A little annoyed with her response, I reminded the nurse: "But I have notified another hospice nurse several times about her leg, but nothing has been done to prevent this from happening." Again, this was another source of frustration for me. Tending to my mother's leg should not have been that difficult.

The warrior spirit in Mom began to fight for her healing. By the second day in the hospital, she was feeling much better, so I decided to take a much-needed vacation to Mexico even though it was difficult for me to leave her. How would she survive in my absence? What if she fell back into a medical slump? Who would be there to save her? The ego is a powerful deterrent to accepting the natural cycles of our lives and in my act of desperation, I adopted a cavalier attitude. I saw myself as the protector, redeemer, and liberator, yet I totally ignored the fact that Mom was blessed with four children and a caring daughter-in-law, and that most of my brothers and my sister-in-law were doing the best that they could. We cared for Mom differently, but our mission was the same. Mom was a major focus for us. My ego and selfish thinking pushed me into deeper levels of loneliness, alienation, and despair day by day. Instead of battling to protect Mom, I fought to be right, barely leaving the door ajar for their suggestions.

Her decline was difficult to see and to accept. Our mother, friend, grandmother, and patient had lived a vibrant life. She pulled herself out of poverty and committed herself to creating a better life for herself and her children. If only I could keep her alive; I didn't want her to leave me. She had been in my life for over sixty years. What would I do? Although we had moments of conflict, she was the rock of the family. She was the matriarch. She was the beautiful, bold Black angel leading us out of states of stress and doubt. But soon I would find myself gathered in a circle of pain and gratefulness watching Mom quietly slip into her new life.

Chapter 23

Simply Sharing

We're fascinated by the words, but where we meet is the silence behind them.

Ram Dass

I was plagued with the thought of Mom's inability to communicate exactly what she was feeling about her illness, especially as her death drew nearer. I knew that she could express her hurt and pain in the moment through her tears, but I wondered what collection of words she would use to describe the life-changing moment of a stroke. She could no longer draw on the language that had helped her maneuver through a segregated world and grow up quickly, rearing four children, to express her joy, pain, and need for change and to survive. I imagine she must have spent many lonely minutes with only her thoughts to keep her company. I wondered whether she somehow spoke to herself.

I believe our words help create our reality. Our words summon change and shape our thoughts and the thoughts of others. Speaking our words helps us release thoughts that otherwise would cause traffic jams in our minds. In Mom's case, I could envision competing thoughts battling for brain space. I could also imagine thoughts fighting to be spoken even though she no longer had the language skills required for full expression.

Without language, Mom had limited self-expression. As she declined, she could not tell anyone how she felt. She could not say if she was afraid or angry. She could not articulate whether she was sad or happy. For someone as engaging as Mom was before her stroke, how did she manage the silence and the loss of self-expression? How did these moments of stillness prepare her for her destiny with death?

Communicating during times of transition, such as facing death, helps to detangle or unbundle the feelings or emotions that we have related to the change. Communicating promotes clarity. Having the ability to simply tell someone else, "I am afraid," is an act of release and surrender. Memories of love and joy are imparted through symbols we learn very early in our lives. The same symbols that I'm sure Mom long had taken for granted were no longer part of her experience. Mom could not draw, read, or speak about her favorite memories of her children or grandchildren. She would have to reflect in silence.

Previous studies show the value of remembrance during the end-of-life transition. In her article, *The Value of Reminiscence in Hospital Care,* Dorothy Wholihan, RN, MSN, OCN, discusses previous findings from researchers R.N. Butler and P.G. Coleman on the value of reminiscence therapy for terminally ill patients. She writes, "Reminiscence Therapy is a simple but effective tool in alleviating some of the emotional problems hospice patients face. By affirming a sense of identity, uniqueness, self-worth, and accomplishment, reminiscence can help patients face death more peacefully."

Notably, reminiscence therapy and life review are techniques used by therapists, especially those with palliative patients, in order to bring value and meaning into a patient's life. According to researchers, it is very common for people to engage in remembering past events from their lives and sharing those memories. The act of reminiscing can enhance the well-being of people experiencing dementia. But Mom could not participate in this type of therapy because her lips were frozen and her thoughts were bound by her condition of silence.

I wonder if there were stories my mother wanted to tell our family but could not. Would her final days have been richer if she could have told her children and grandchildren more about growing up in a shotgun house on stilts and remembering the loving support she received from her mother-in-law, Martha Helen Jordan, as she began her married life in Cincinnati in 1951? I wish I knew what additional support Mom needed from me. Was there a way I could have made her end-of-life journey more joyful or less fearful? It pains me to know that she could not tell her story through words.

I remember sitting outside with Mom one summer afternoon as I played music for her. I often played church hymns on YouTube to ease the moments. The music also tested Mom's memory; I would carefully watch to see if she sang along with the words. I knew that the stroke damaged portions of her brain, and it was clear that she suffered some short-term and long-term memory loss. Listening to the music, talking about pleasant memories, and having lovely moments with my mother was also comforting to me. I, too, benefitted from this simple kind of reminiscence therapy.

That afternoon I asked Mom, "Do you ever think about Big Mamma?"—her grandmother. My hope was that the music would transport her back in time, sparking memories of Big Mamma. Immediately, Mom's normal and rather blank facial expression shifted to an expression of sorrow. She began to cry. Her tears confirmed to me that her long-term memory was still active. At the same time, the intensity of her tears also confirmed that Big Mamma was a tremendous influence in her life. I knew that Big Mamma helped raise my mother, but I was curious about what she was thinking in the moment. What more could she have said if she could speak? I could have asked her why she was crying, but her limited language would have created confusion and frustration for her.

A popular communication theory I learned as an undergraduate student was that it is impossible to not communicate. Several researchers insisted that we are always in a mode of communicating, even when we are not speaking. Communication occurs through facial expression and body language. For example, crossing my arms in a meeting might be perceived as a posture of defensiveness or a barrier to hearing the ideas of others. If someone passes me on the street, without saying even one word, that person is still communicating something to me.

Our family relied heavily on Mom's tears, facial expressions, and the tone and volume of her articulations. She communicated, but much of the meaning was lost because she had no language we could understand. We were constantly guessing Mom's needs, wishes, and desires. There were times when we guessed correctly, but there were many times when we did not. As she slowly slipped away, it was even more difficult to decipher the images and thoughts my mother had in her mind. I had to trust that her faith minimized some of her fears and that the love she felt from us was a reminder that she was not alone.

As Mom transitioned to the next life unable to communicate her feelings, so the family would have to begin to shift to a world without her. We walked the road of change with her, not knowing what her death would personally mean for each of us. We each would have our own stories to tell. I remember my younger brother sharing a beautiful memory the evening of Mom's passing. He had seen a deer right outside the window of Mom's condominium. The deer stood still, facing Mom's front porch, looking in my brother's direction. It was not unusual to see deer on the property, but my brother was drawn to this deer for some reason. He told me that after standing still for a few minutes, the deer slowly walked away towards the woods. My brother felt a strong connection to Mom through the deer. The message the deer had for him was that Mom was at peace. He told me he felt so much better after the experience. I believe in the silence of that moment, Mom was still communicating in her own unique way from the afterlife, not with words, but through God's creation, nature.

Chapter 24

Mortality

*Even after all of this time, the Sun never says to the
Earth, "You owe me." Look what happens with a love
like that. It lights up the sky.*

Hafiz

 hat is this place? The room is dripping with sadness.
Nestled in Mom's arms, I look around to see Aunt
Lynne and Fay and Uncle Butch sitting in the church pews looking forlorn. I can feel their despondency. As if it were a cave, I
recall silence and stillness in this somber place. Close to Mom's
heart, I feel protected from any possible emerging doom. She car-
ries me to the front of the building, moving closer and closer to
the wooden box.

Feelings of anticipation can be overwhelming, especially when
you are very young and begin to realize that you are no longer the
center of the universe. There are other lives besides your own that
exist in your circle. So, I continue to look around, trying to figure
out the moment as we move closer to the box. I look down, still feeling the warmth of Mom's embrace. And behold. Stretched out in

the box is a dark-brown-skinned man. His eyes are closed. He is not moving. No breath. Frozen in time. But then I remember no more. I cannot remember whether I cry, stare, or jump from fear. I do not remember anything else about seeing death for the first time.

Sixty years later, I can still remember my first encounter with death. At the age of two or three, it was a haunting moment. Mom always expressed her surprise that I could remember this event. "Cheryl," she would say, "that was either Uncle Casey's or my stepfather's funeral. My stepfather died in 1957! How can you remember? You were only about two when he died." Her disbelief made me question myself. Did I make this story up? Was it a bad dream? How could I remember the funeral? How could I sense the sadness? Years later, I would eventually recognize my empath tendencies and a natural calling for me to feel deeply.

To this day, I believe my fear of dying is related to this event. The funeral was too much for me to process. I am sure Mom didn't think I would remember what was going on at the time, so I cannot blame her. How many people can remember when they were two or three years old? Honoring the dead in the Black community is a celebratory occasion full of pomp and circumstance. Attendees revel in salvation and glory for the departed, as the choir sings the songs of Zion, and the officiating pastor reminds us that we are just "passing through." It is a family affair and a "homegoing." All family members are expected to attend, regardless of how far away they live. In that particular case, it did not matter if it was Uncle Casey or stepdaddy Dallas; Mom had to go home to show her respect.

More than sixty years later, my body is arrested and relaxed, suspended 32,000 feet in the air, returning from Mexico to eventually plan a homegoing for Mom. My son's life partner,

Carlos, planned this trip for himself and his mother, Iman and me, to venture to the warm waters of the Pacific Ocean. Hesitant about leaving Mom, I also knew it was important for me to surround myself with Iman's love and the positive energy that would come from being in the presence of Carlos and Carlos's mother. I finally convinced myself that Aunt Fay would be there to support my brother and sister-in-law with taking care of Mom and once I knew that she would provide support to my brother and his wife, my fears about leaving for five days disappeared. Now, returning home from Mexico weepy and fatigued, I sat next to the nicest young man. I welcomed his conversation and positive sentiments. His energy soothed my shattered spirit and made me forget for brief seconds what would face me once I arrived at the assisted living facility.

A little over a week after leaving Mexico, Mom lay lifeless, surrounded in a circle of love. With a whisper from Jackie who was sitting at Mom's bedside, family members and friends were quietly summoned to the bedside for prayer. A friend of the family, Jackie flew from Maryland to Ohio to provide support. As a registered nurse, she was an astute observer of her surroundings and a change master. Always rising to the challenge, her swift actions could never be defeated. She gave unconditionally. She was an anchor for my brother and a torch of bright healing light for the rest of our family, especially during this time of grief and fear. Jackie stayed connected to our hearts with her comforting words, which could soothe the soul of anyone in pain. I wonder if Mom knew that Jackie was by her side. I wonder if Jackie's love gave Mom the courage to release, to exhale, to depart.

On that sad day, Mom's hair was straight and the brightest white. She wore the new brown, beige, and black top with an abstract pattern that she wanted to wear for a special occasion. I recalled the moment I showed her the top that I had recently purchased. I tried to get her to wear it several days after buying it, but she refused. Sometimes I wonder if she was waiting for this special day and moment to wear it.

Jean Jordan departed this earth on September 7, 2018. Her body was tired, but her energy for living never wavered during her illness until shortly before her death. Even as she became weaker and weaker each day, I could not forget the power of her words as a loving mother and the strength of her love—not only for me but also for her sons, daughter-in-law, sisters, brother, and grandchildren.

It was a tender moment to see my mother's care for others reciprocated as she was circled by family, friends, and healthcare professionals. I cannot help but believe that she timed her death, just like she planned everything else in her life. A few days before she died, a physician friend of my brother's encouraged the family to whisper funny stories or secret mischievous deeds from the past in her ear. We heard that hearing would be the last sense to leave her. He also encouraged us to let Mom know how much she was loved and to thank her for being such a tremendous force in our lives.

To this day, I am not sure when Mom took her last breath. Sometimes I ask myself, does it really matter? For the duration of her illness, I had been obsessed with knowing every detail regarding Mom's care. And even now, I continued to need to know and understand the nuances and intricacies of her passing. Questions consumed me: What is Mom thinking right now? Does she know she is dying? Is she concerned about leaving the family? Is she afraid? Even months later, I was curious about the specific circumstances of her transition. My need to protect her from suffering and doubt was the guiding principle of my care of her.

I kept thinking about how grateful I was for Jean Jordan. I lay by her side gently caressing her hand, and I was happy to see her surrounded by love and prayer as she gently took her last breath. The shine of her love left us with a glow even during a time of loss. Although I could not interpret her last whispers to me as she drifted away, my heart told me she was saying, "Be strong, my precious princess, help keep the family together, and you are the best daughter I could ever have."

That September 7, I was reminded that we cannot escape death, but we *can* create a legacy of love that extends beyond generations. How we live our lives is what matters. We must embrace *ubuntu* thoughts. Life matters when we learn to surrender, to forgive, and to let go of guilt. Sometimes there are some forces we cannot fight. When we let go and live joyfully in the moment, our lives are enriched. My life was enriched during this ride. And although it was a ride of a lifetime, I knew one day *I* would rest peacefully because I know I did my best for Mom.

Chapter 25

Not an Anomaly

*Empathy is forgetting oneself in the joys and sorrows of
another, so much so that you actually feel that the joy or
sorrow experienced by another is your own joy and sorrow. Empathy involves complete identification
with another.*

Dada Vaswani

I was anxious to visit Mom's mausoleum one more time
before I left Cincinnati to drive back to Atlanta. A year had
passed since Mom's passing, so I was determined to get to the cemetery. I was happy that my brother decided to join me and my dog
Parker, to visit Mom's final resting place. Her crypt was inside a
mausoleum in a 175-year-old, 700-acre cemetery designated as a
National Historical Landmark. Several years before Mom's stroke,
I remember a co-worker of mine telling me about the legacy of
Spring Grove Cemetery. As the third largest cemetery in the coun-
try, Spring Grove's design was inspired by cemeteries in Paris,
France, and Cambridge, Massachusetts, and it featured beautiful

Gothic buildings, landscaping, and meandering paths anchored by small lakes with miniature cascading waterfalls.

The cemetery was not only a final resting place for Mom, but also where the remains of abolitionists and anti-slavery activists lie—people like Salmon P. Chase, a defender of enslaved fugitives, John McLean, a Supreme Court Justice and defender for civil rights in the infamous Dred Scott vs. Sandford case, and Catharine and Levi Coffin, organizers of the Cincinnati Underground Railroad. The cemetery is also an arboretum and educational facility for horticulture enthusiasts.

Founded in 1844, Black Cincinnatians were not buried there originally. During that same year, the United American Cemetery, the first reputable cemetery for Black Cincinnatians, was founded. My father, grandparents, aunts, uncles, and a host of other relatives are buried there, but Mom chose Spring Grove Cemetery as the new home for her physical body.

We arrived at the cemetery in the early afternoon. We drove up to the front of one of several mausoleums in Spring Grove. Mom's crypt was located on the second row from the ground, and three rows of crypts stood above her row. I was amazed again by the breathtaking view and the proximity of the mausoleum to a lake surrounded by many trees, now barren from the cold midwestern winter. I watched swans dip their heads in and out of the water, sometimes forming the shape of a heart as they greeted each other. I knew Mom would be pleased.

My brother, Parker, and I got out of the car and stood close to Mom's crypt. I looked at her name written in bronze letters affixed to the marble wall. Seeing her name, year of birth, and year of death reminded me that she was gone. I could not escape my feelings of sadness and longing for her. I rubbed my right hand across the letters of her name as if she could feel the sensation of my touch. Out of nowhere, Parker began to whimper, something he seldom does. Astonished, I looked at my brother and said, "Parker is crying! He must know that Mom is close by." My brother, a science guy who wanted a telescope at the age of twelve, had doubts.

We moved to another wall of crypts nearby, and Parker did not make a sound. Yet when we slowly walked back to Mom's crypt, Parker began to cry again. What was happening? Did Parker intuitively sense our grief? Or could he smell Mom's scent? I left the cemetery still in shock. I took my brother home and decided to drive by the cemetery again before I began the drive to Atlanta. I had to know if Parker's response was just an anomaly. But it was not. As soon as we got out of the car and stood in front of my mom's crypt, Parker, my fourteen-year-old poodle mixed with dachshund began to cry again. Parker not only knew my heart but knew my mother's as well. I tried to imagine another explanation for his behavior. And I couldn't help but consider the possibility that Mom was trying to tell us that she was sorry and saddened she had to leave us through Parker. My rational mind, on the other hand, kept insisting that this was just a coincidence. Although I believe that miracles do exist and that spiritual energy is real, we tend to push mystical phenomena that we cannot explain out of our minds. Yet the third whimper from Parker was confirmation enough for me that he was feeling something related to Mom when he was near her crypt.

Years later, I remain convinced that my mother was communicating with me via Parker that afternoon. Parker was helping my mother proclaim the power of her love for us even from the grave. He shared a message from my mother a year after her death.

Visiting Mom with Parker was an extraordinary moment. Leaving the cemetery, I thought about what I had just experienced. It reminded me of the exhilaration of the wind on my face as we rode that roller coaster called "The Beast" forty-five years ago, even though I was paralyzed with fear. Similarly, I felt freedom from my sorrow because I was so enthralled by what Parker was offering me. His gift reminded me of how connected living beings are. I was mystified, relieved, and melancholy all at the same time as I drove south toward Atlanta with my beloved dog at my side. In that moment, I had no choice but to start my life over again.

Citations

Introduction: Cleage, Pearl, "What Looks Like Crazy on an Ordinary Day,"(2012):4

Chapter 1: Unknown, https://thepositiveedge.net/2021/01/02/looking-back-to-help-us-look-forward/

Chapter 2: Jordan, Cheryl (2022)

Chapter 3: King, Martin Luther Jr., "I Have a Dream: Writings and Speeches That Changed the World," https://www.goodreads.com/work/quotes/1618365-i-have-a-dream-writings-and-speeches-that-changed-the-world [accessed November 1, 2022]

Chapter 4: https://www.thepeoplesheart.org/ubuntu/calling-our-ancestors/ [accessed November 1, 2022]

Chapter 5: https://www.goodreads.com/quotes/9407252-there-is-in-this-world-no-such-force-as-the [accessed November 1, 2022]

Chapter 6: Nepo, Mark, The Book of Awakening: Having the Life You Want by Being Present to the Life You Have, " (1999)

Chapter 7: Unknown, https://proverbicals.com/guilt [accessed November 1, 2022]

Chapter 8: Giovanni, Nikki, https://www.goodreads.com/quotes/437864-deal-with-yourself-as-a-individual-worthy-of-respect-and [accessed November 1, 2022]

Chapter 9: Charlayne Hunter-Gault , "Remembering Desmond Tutu's Hope, (December 27, 2021), https://www.newyorker.com/news/postscript/remembering-desmond-tutus-hope [accessed November 1, 2022]

Chapter 10: Baldwin, James, Peck, Raul, & Jackson, Samuel, "I Am Not Your Negro Documentary," (2017)

Chapter 11: May, Kate, "I am, because of you: Further Reading on Ubuntu, " (December 31, 2013), https://blog.ted.com/further-reading-on-ubuntu/ [accessed November 1, 2022]

Chapter 12: Lagace', Maxime, https://wisdomquotes.com/friendship-quotes/ [accessed November 1, 2022]

Chapter 13: Frantzces, Lys, "40 Quotes From Incredible Black Women That Will Inspire You To Keep Going," (July 29, 2022) https://www.blackgirlventures.org/post/40-quotes-from-incredible-black-women-that-will-inspire-you-to-keep-going [accessed November 1, 2022]

Chapter 14: Matt. 6:33 (KJV)

Chapter 15: https://historicalsnaps.com/2020/11/24/sojourner-truth-life-is-a-hard-battle-anyway/ [accessed November 2, 2022]

Chapter 16: *Unknown*

Chapter 17: Mafi, Marham and Kolin, Azima, "Rumi's Little Book of Life: The Garden of the Soul, the Heart and the Spirit," (2012)

Chapter 18: Douglas, Arthur, "928 Maya Angelou Quotes," (2019):107

Chapter 20: Osbon, Diane, "Reflections on the Art of Living: A Joseph Campbell Companion"(1991)

Chapter 21: Gorman, Amanda, "The Hill We Climb," President Inauguration (excerpt from speech, Washington D.C., January 20, 2021)

Chapter 22: Keller, Helen, "We Bereaved," (1929)

Chapter 23: Dass, Ram, "Be Here Now," https://www.findcenter.com/quote/45123/were-fascinated-by-the-words-but-where-we-meet-is-in-the-silence-behind-them/more?pageno=3 [accessed November 2, 2022]

Chapter 24: Ladinsky, Daniel, "The Gift: Poems Written by Hafiz The Great Sufi Master," (August 1, 1999)

About the Author

Cheryl Jordan is the founder of U.magine Performance Consulting. She is a certified professional diversity executive coach and leadership development consultant. She's presented internationally on the topic of women in leadership and diversity and inclusion. Based on her research on identifying the strategies Black women executives use to excel in the workplace, Cheryl developed a women's leadership framework for overcoming bias and marginalization. She's been a mentor to numerous women leaders searching for meaning, fulfillment, and self-actualization in their personal and professional lives. Cheryl currently resides in Atlanta, GA.

In 2016, Cheryl temporarily relocated from Atlanta to her hometown of Cincinnati, Ohio, to help care for her mom after her mom experienced a life-changing illness. Operating in a space of trauma for almost three years as a primary caregiver, Cheryl's mom's illness eventually shifted her perspective on the meaning of living a rich and fulfilled life, on the power of love as an agent for personal change, and on the acceptance of things she could not control as she witnessed her mom slowly lose her fight with her mortality. She highlights her personal journey of navigating pain, finding joy, and releasing what she could not control during her mom's illness. Cheryl's intimate story is a testimony of what anyone can experience when faced with trauma and portrays an alchemy for finding moments to learn to breathe again.

Made in the USA
Columbia, SC
20 April 2023